SPECTACULAR

SOUTH AFRICA

SPECTACULAR

SOUTH AFRICA

TIM O'HAGAN

picture credits

AI=Africa Imagery; DR=David Rogers; FK=Fanie Kloppers; GC=Gerald Cubitt; GI=Gallo Images; GW= Graeme Williams; HvH=Hein von Hörsten; IOA=Images of Africa; iAP=iAfrika Photos; IM=Ivor Migdoll; JdP= Jéan du Plessis; JJ=Jeremy Jowell; JR=John Robinson; KB=Karl Beath; LE=Leopard Enterprises; LH=Lex Hes; LS=Lionel Soule; LvH=Lanz von Hörsten; MA= Mike Allwood; MS=Mark Skinner; NDWP=Nigel Dennis Wildlife Photography; NJD=Nigel J Dennis; PA=Photo Access; PW=Patrick Wagner; RdlH=Roger de la Harpe; SA= Shaen Adey; SP=South Photographs; WK=Walter Knirr; WL= Wicus Leeuwner

Cover: WK; **pages 1:** MA/NDWP; **2:** DR; **3:** SA; **4:** RdlH/GI (top), FK/LE (bottom); **5:** JJ (top left), WL (top middle), HvH/IOA (top right), SA/IOA (bottom left), HvH (bottom right); **8:** SA/IOA; **9:** WK; **10:** SA; **11:** LS; **12:** MS; **13:** Benny Gool/Trace; **14:** Keith Young; **15:** MS/PA; **16:** Chad Henning/Cape Photo Library; **17:** SA; **18:** MS/PA; **19:** SA/GI; **20–1:** SA; **22–3:** LvH; **24–6:** Eric Miller/iAP; **27:** Johann van Tonder/ PictureNET Africa; **28:** LvH/GI; **29:** SA; **30:** LvH; **31:** MS/PA; **32:** MS/PA; **33:** LS; **34:** HvH/IOA; **35:** WK; **36:** GC; **37–9:** WK; **40:** LvH; **41:** HvH/GI; **42:** MA/NDWP; **43:** Anthony Johnson/IOA; **44–6:** LvH; **47:** HvH; **48:** JdP; **49:** GC; **50:** HvH; **51:** LvH; **52:** SA/IOA; **53:** JJ/iAP; **54:** JdP; **55:** WK; **56:** LvH; **57:** WK; **58:** Koos Delport/PA; **59:** LvH; **60:** WK; **61:** LvH; **62:** WK; **63:** HvH; **64:** PW/Getaway/PA; **65:** KB; **66:** GC; **67:** NJD/AI; **68:** WL; **69–71:** HvH; **72:** WK; **73:** DR; **74:** WK; **75:** NJD/AI; **76:** SA; **77–78:** LvH; **79–80:** HvH; **81:** HvH/ IOA; **82:** WK; **83:** HvH/IOA; **84:** Philip Schedler; **85:** JdP/ Cape Photo Library; **86–87:** HvH/IOA; **88:** SA/IOA; **89:** DR; **90–1:** KB; **92–4:** SA/IOA; **95:** JR/IOA; **96:** GC; **97:** SA/ IOA; **98:** IM; **99:** RdlH/AI; **100:** Michael Brett; **101:** RdlH/ AI; **102:** SA/IOA; **103–5:** WK; **106:** SA/IOA; **107:** SA/GI; **108:** NJD/IOA; **109:** SA/IOA; **110:** WK; **111:** DR; **112:** SA/IOA; **113:** RdlH/AI; **114:** RdlH/IOA; **115:** SA/IOA; **116:** LvH; **117:** DR; **118:** RdlH/GI; **119:** SA/IOA; **120:** HvH; **121:** LvH; **122:** DR/Getaway/PA; **123:** HvH; **124:** I vH; **125:** Heinrich van den Berg/HPH Photography; **126:** WK; **127:** HvH; **128–9:** WK; **130–1:** HvH; **132:** David Bristow/ Getaway/PA; **133:** WK; **134:** PW/ Getaway/PA; **135:** FK/ LE; **136–7:** WK; **138:** LH; **139:** LvH/IOA; **140:** NJD/AI; **141:** Ingrid van den Berg/HPH Photography; **142:** NJD/ GI; **143:** LH; **144:** SA/IOA; **145:** LvH/IOA; **146–7:** WK; **148:** SA/IOA; **149:** WK; **150:** SA/South African National Roads Agency Limited; **151:** WK; **152–6:** SA/IOA; **157:** WK/IOA; **158:** GW/SP; **159:** WK/PA; **160–3:** SA/ IOA; **164:** Paul Velasco/GI; **165:** JJ; **166:** WK/IOA; **167:** SA/IOA; **168:** Lorna Stanton/GI; **169:** WK/IOA; **170–1:** SA/IOA; **172:** LvH/GI; **173:** WK; **174 & 175:** LvH; **176:** WK.

Struik Publishers
(a division of New Holland Publishing (South Africa) (Pty) Ltd)
New Holland Publishing is a member of Johnnic Communications Ltd

Struik House
80 McKenzie Street
Cape Town 8001
South Africa

Garfield House
86-88 Edgware Road
London W2 2EA
United Kingdom

14 Aquatic Drive
Frenchs Forest
NSW 2086

218 Lake Road
Northcote
Auckland

First edition 2001
Second edition 2004

ISBN-13: 978-1-770070-81-3
ISBN-10: 1-7700770-81-8
10 9 8 7 6 5 4 3 2

Website: www.struik.co.za
Please email comments or updates to: The Editor, Spectacular South Africa, updates@struik.co.za

Copyright © 2001, 2004 in published edition and map: Struik Publishers
Copyright © 2001, 2004 in text: Tim O'Hagan
Copyright © 2001, 2004 in photographs:
As credited on this page

Designer: Janice Evans
Publishing manager: Annlerie van Rooyen
Editor: Lesley Hay-Whitton
French translator: Jean-Paul Houssière
German translator: Friedel Herrmann
Cartographer: Steven Felmore
Proofreader: Glynne Newlands

Reproduction by Hirt & Carter Cape (Pty) Ltd
Printed and bound by Ajanta Offset

www.imagesofafrica.co.za

IMAGES OF AFRICA
PHOTO LIBRARY

FRONT COVER: Baobab, Messina

HALF TITLE: Spring flowers, Clanwilliam

TITLE PAGE: Snow-capped mountains, Little Karoo (LEFT), Table Mountain, Cape Town (RIGHT)

OPPOSITE PAGE: Hindu temple dancer (TOP), Cape minstrel (BOTTOM)

THIS PAGE: West Coast fisherman (TOP LEFT), Namaqualand woman and child (TOP MIDDLE), Xhosa woman, Lesedi (ABOVE), Zulu beadwork (FAR LEFT), Ndebele woman (LEFT)

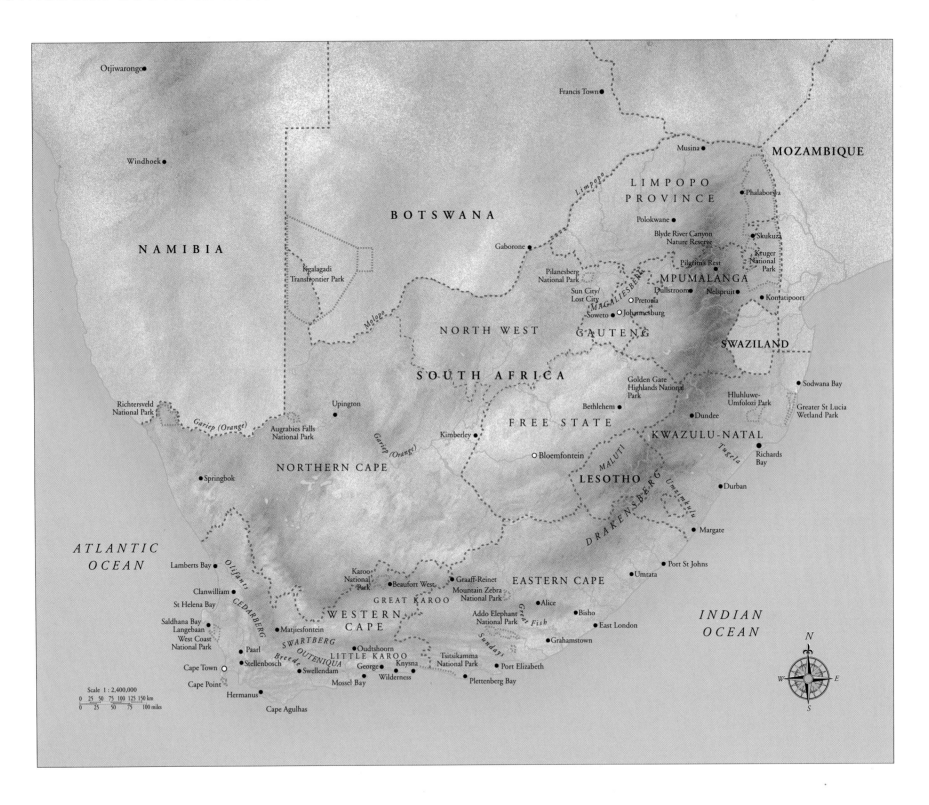

Otjiwarongo

Francis Town

MOZAMBIQUE

Musina

LIMPOPO
PROVINCE

Windhoek

Limpopo

Phalaborwa

BOTSWANA

Polokwane

NAMIBIA

Blyde River Canyon
Nature Reserve

Skukuza

Gaborone

Pilgrim's Rest

Kruger
National
Park

Kgalagadi
Transfrontier Park

Pilanesberg
National Park

MPUMALANGA

Sun City/
Lost City

Dullstroom

Nelspruit

Komatipoort

MAGALIESBERG

Pretoria

Molopo

NORTH WEST

GAUTENG

Soweto

Johannesburg

SWAZILAND

SOUTH AFRICA

Golden Gate
Highlands National
Park

Sodwana Bay

Richtersveld
National Park

Gariep (Orange)

Upington

Bethlehem

Hluhluwe-
Umfolozi Park

Greater St Lucia
Wetland Park

Augrabies Falls
National Park

FREE STATE

Dundee

*Gariep
(Orange)*

Kimberley

KWAZULU-NATAL

Bloemfontein

Richards
Bay

Springbok

NORTHERN CAPE

MALUTI

LESOTHO

Durban

Umzimkulu

Tugela

DRAKENSBERG

Margate

ATLANTIC
OCEAN

Port St Johns

Lamberts Bay

Olifants

Karoo
National
Park

Umtata

Clanwilliam

CEDARBERG

GREAT KAROO

Graaff-Reinet

EASTERN CAPE

St Helena Bay

Beaufort West

Mountain Zebra
National Park

Alice

INDIAN
OCEAN

Saldanha Bay
Langebaan
West Coast
National Park

Matjiesfontein

Addo Elephant
National Park

Great Fish

Bisho

East London

SWARTBERG

Paarl

OUTENIQUA

LITTLE KAROO

Grahamstown

Stellenbosch

Oudtshoorn

Tsitsikamma
National Park

Cape Town

Breede

Swellendam

George

Knysna

Port Elizabeth

Cape Point

Mossel Bay

Wilderness

Plettenberg Bay

Sundays

Hermanus

Scale 1 : 2,400,000

0   25   50   75   100   125 150 km

0   25   50   75   100 miles

Cape Agulhas

N

W   E

S

Like a mighty bulwark in the southern seas, South Africa stands at the end of the Dark Continent, a cosmopolitan country whose natural wonders have few peers on earth. At its tip a fynbos-covered peninsula snakes into the wilderness of two mighty oceans, a beacon as enigmatic and beautiful as the country it announces. To the east the warm Indian Ocean caresses a coastline of copper sands, forests and bush-fringed dunes, interspersed with seaside villages and major ports. To the west the icy Atlantic pummels a coastline of quaint hamlets and fishing villages leading to a semi-desert hinterland of gravel plains, dry river beds and bizarre rock formations. Between the two is a land of plenty, a kaleidoscope of contrasting cultures, where bustling cities and towns, glittering casino resorts and rustic villages lie on the doorstep of great game parks and nature reserves populated by a huge array of mammals, birds and insects. From the dunes of the Kalahari to the rainforests of Tsitsikamma, from the turrets of the Drakensberg to the sands of the Wild Coast, South Africa is a paradise of sights and sounds, with all the trappings of a first-world country. Urban five-star hotels and restaurants compete with ethnic country kraals for the custom of visitors from around the world. Xhosa and Zulu crafts sold on the pavements of Cape Town and Durban attract as much interest as the upmarket shopping malls of Johannesburg and Pretoria. This is South Africa, the pedestal of Africa, a place with a fascinating mix of cultures, where people come to savour nature at its best. Whether you're ascending the majestic flanks of Table Mountain, watching rhino in a game reserve or peering into the awesome amphitheatre of the Blyde River Canyon, you'll know you've arrived — in the most spectacular land on earth.

Située à la pointe du Continent noir, l'Afrique du Sud est un pays cosmopolite, dont les merveilles naturelles n'ont que peu d'égales sur cette terre. A son extrémité, une péninsule recouverte d'une flore unique, pénètre en serpentant dans l'immensité sauvage de deux océans. Vers l'est, les eaux chaudes de l'océan Indien baignent un littoral aux sables dorés, bordé de forêts et parsemé de petits villages et de ports importants. A l'ouest, les vagues glacées de l'Atlantique pilonnent une côte où se nichent hameaux pittoresques et villages de pêcheurs, entourés de plaines désertiques et d'extraordinaires formations rocheuses. Entre les deux se niche un pays de cocagne, un kaléidoscope de cultures variées, où villes animées et hameaux somnolents sont à la lisière de réserves naturelles, abritant une énorme variété de mammifères, d'oiseaux et d'insectes. Des dunes du Kalahari aux forêts subtropicales du Tsitsikamma, des tourelles du Drakensberg aux sables de la Wild Coast, l'Afrique du Sud est un véritable éden. Hôtels de haute gamme et restaurants chics font la concurrence avec les kraals ethniques de la campagne pour attirer des visiteurs venant du monde entier. L'art des Xhosas et des Zoulous, vendu à même les trottoirs de Cape Town et de Durban, attire tout autant l'attention que les centres commerciaux les plus élégants de Johannesburg et de Pretoria. Ceci est l'Afrique du Sud, le socle du continent africain, une région contenant une étonnante diversité de cultures, où se retrouvent ceux qui recherchent les merveilles de la nature. Que vous escaladiez les flancs imposants de Table Mountain, observiez les rhinocéros dans une réserve naturelle ou encore admiriez le spectacle majestueux de Blyde River Canyon, vous saurez que vous êtes arrivés dans le pays le plus spectaculaire du monde.

Wie ein mächtiges Bollwerk in den südlichen Ozeanen, bildet Südafrika den Endpunkt des Dunklen Kontinents – ein kosmopolitisches Land, dessen prachtvolle Natur nur wenig Ebenbürtiges auf der Erde findet. An der Spitze ragt eine Halbinsel in das ungestüme Meer. Im Osten streichelt der warme Indische Ozean einen Küstenstreifen mit Sandstränden, Wäldern und bewachsenen Dünen, unterbrochen von kleinen Küstenorten und wichtigen Hafenstädten. Im Westen rollen die Brecher des kalten Atlantik an eine Küste mit malerischen Ortschaften und Fischerdörfern, die übergeht in eine Halbwüste mit Geröllebenen, ausgetrockneten Flußläufen und bizarren Felsformationen. Zwischen den Ozeanen erstreckt sich ein Land der Fülle, ein Kaleidoskop unterschiedlicher Kulturen, wo geschäftige Städte, schillernde Kasinos und rustikale Dörfer an der Schwelle zu riesigen Wildparks und Naturschutzgebieten liegen. Von den Dünen der Kalahari bis zu den Wäldern des Tsitsikamma, von den Felstürmen der Drakensberge bis zu den Sandstränden der Wildküste – Südafrika bietet eine paradiesische Vielfalt für Auge und Ohr und gleichzeitig alle Annehmlichkeiten der Zivilisation. Fünf-Sterne-Hotels und Restaurants in den Stadtgebieten wetteifern mit ethnischen Kraals um die Gunst der Besucher aus aller Welt. Straßenstände in Kapstadt und Durban rufen genauso Interesse hervor wie elegante Einkaufspassagen in Johannesburg und Pretoria. Dies ist Südafrika, die Bühne Afrikas, wo sich ein faszinierendes Spiel der Kulturen präsentiert, und wo Menschen hinreisen, um die Natur in ihrer ganzen Schönheit zu erleben. Ob auf dem Tafelberg oder im Wildpark oder am Blyde River Cañon – es durchpulst Sie das Gefühl, angekommen zu sein – im großartigsten Land der Welt.

THE FAIREST CAPE

Like a benign sandstone giant, Table Mountain towers above the sprawl of central Cape Town and its satellite suburbs, which curl around Devil's Peak to the east and Lion's Head to the north-west (ABOVE). Visible from 200 kilometres out at sea, Table Mountain once served as a navigation beacon for Portuguese explorers. Today it is a mecca for tourists, who reach the 1,086-metre summit by cable-car (OPPOSITE).

TABLE MOUNTAIN CABLEWAY

Comme un géant bienveillant, Table Mountain domine Cape Town et ses faubourgs, qui, vers l'est contournent Devil's Peak, et au nord ouest, Lion's Head (CI-CONTRE). Table Mountain est visible à 200 kilomètres au large, et servait autrefois de repère aux explorateurs portugais. De nos jours, la montagne est la Mecque des touristes qui peuvent atteindre son sommet à 1,086 mètres, par téléférique (CI-DESSUS).

Wie ein wohlwollender Riese aus Sandstein, beherrscht der Tafelberg das Häusermeer von Kapstadt und Vororten, das sich um Teufelsspitze und Löwenkopf (GEGENÜBER) gruppiert. Vom Meer aus einer Entfernung von über 200km wahrzunehmen, war der Tafelberg einst eine wichtige Navigationshilfe für die Entdeckungsreisenden. Heute ist er ein Mekka für Touristen, die den 1,086m hohen Gipfel mit der Seilbahn erreichen (OBEN).

DOCKSIDE MAGIC

The maritime delights of the Victoria and Alfred Waterfront (ABOVE) lure visitors from all over the world. Attractions range from lavish cuisine at the water's edge to a huge array of entertainment and shopping options. Visitors pack out the Waterfront's open-air Agfa Amphitheatre for a night-time symphony concert (OPPOSITE).

WATERFRONT SYMPHONY

L'atmosphère maritime du Victoria and Alfred Waterfront (CI-CONTRE) attire les visiteurs du monde entier. On y trouve des restaurants à la gastronomie somptueuse, de nombreux magasins et un grand choix de spectacles. Les visiteurs s'attroupent à l'Agfa Amphithéâtre pour une soirée de concert en plein air (CI-DESSUS).

Die maritim geprägten Reize der Victoria und Alfred Waterfront (GEGENÜBER) locken Besucher aus aller Welt. Es wird viel geboten: von großzügigen Speiseangeboten mit Blick aufs Wasser bis zu vielfältigen Unterhaltungs- und Einkaufsmöglichkeiten. Das Publikum im vollbesetzten Agfa-Freiluft-Theater genießt ein nächtliches Symphoniekonzert (OBEN).

ROBBEN ISLAND

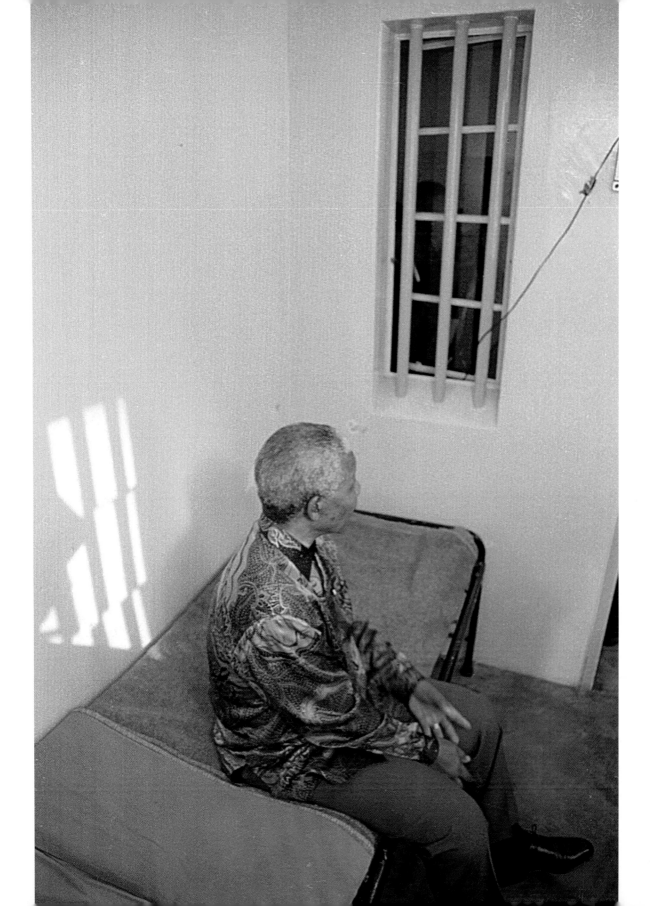

MANDELA'S CELL

Robben Island, where Nelson Mandela spent most of his 27 years in prison, lies tantalisingly close to the mainland, basking in the blue canvas of the Atlantic (OPPOSITE). Mandela revisits the tiny cell in which he was incarcerated (LEFT).

Robben Island, entourée des flots bleus de l'Atlantique (CI-CONTRE), où Nelson Mandela passa la plupart de ses 27 ans d'incarcération. L'île prison, cruellement, touche presque le continent. Mandela revisite la minuscule cellule dans laquelle il était prisonnier (À GAUCHE).

Robbeneiland, wo Nelson Mandela die längste Zeit seiner 27jährigen Inhaftierung zugebracht hat, liegt in aufreizender Nähe des Festlandes, eingebettet in die blaue Seelandschaft des Atlantik (GEGENÜBER). Mandela stattet der winzigen Zelle, wo er einmal eingekerkert war, einen Besuch ab (LINKS).

13

CHANGING OF THE GUARD

A Guard Corps, dressed in 17th century-style uniforms, struts out proudly (ABOVE) during a ceremonial changing of the guard within the pentagonal walls of South Africa's oldest building, the Castle of Good Hope. A short distance away, the imposing sandstone edifice of the Renaissance-style City Hall, built in 1905, towers above the bustling flea markets of the Grand Parade (OPPOSITE).

CITY HALL

Un régiment de gardes en uniforme du 17ième (CI-CONTRE), marche fièrement lors d'une relève de la garde entre les murs du Castle of Good Hope, le plus ancien édifice en Afrique du Sud. A deux pas, l'imposant Hôtel de Ville en style renaissance, érigé en 1905, domine la 'Grand Parade' et ses marchés aux puces animés (À DROITE).

Ein Wachbataillon, uniformiert wie im 17. Jahrhundert, marschiert stolz (GEGENÜBER) bei einer zeremoniellen Wachablösung innerhalb der sternförmigen Festungsmauern von Südafrikas ältestem Bauwerk, dem Kastell der Guten Hoffnung. Ganz in der Nähe steht das beeindruckende, ehemalige Rathaus, ein Sandsteingebäude im Renaissancestil von 1905, das jetzt auf den geschäftigen Flohmarkt hinabblickt, der den alten Exerzierplatz mit Leben erfüllt (RECHTS).

FLOWERS ON PARADE

A flower seller with fragrant bouquets of St Joseph's lilies and carnations at the Grand Parade (LEFT). A vendor at the Salt River Market (OPPOSITE) offers a mouth-watering selection of fresh vegetables and subtropical fruits.

Une marchande de fleurs offre ses bouquets de lys et d'œillets odorants sur la 'Grand Parade' (À GAUCHE). Au Salt River Market (CI-CONTRE), on trouvera un grand choix de légumes et fruits subtropicaux de qualité.

Eine Blumenhändlerin bietet auf dem ehemaligen Exerzierplatz duftende Sträuße von Josefslilien und Nelken an (LINKS). Frisches Gemüse und die schönen, subtropischen Früchte werden von einer Händlerin auf dem Salt River Market feilgehalten (GEGENÜBER).

FRUIT FOR AFRICA

GREENMARKET SQUARE

AFRICAN IMAGE CURIO SHOP

Arts and crafts stalls on Greenmarket Square (OPPOSITE). African wares lure visitors to curio shops like this one off Greenmarket Square (ABOVE).

Les échoppes au marché d'artisanat de Greenmarket Square (CI-CONTRE). Les articles africains attirent les visiteurs dans les magasins de souvenirs (CI-DESSUS).

Stände auf dem Greenmarket Square (GEGENÜBER). Afrikanische Kunst lockt die Besucher in Souvenirgeschäfte wie diesen am Greenmarket Square (OBEN).

CHURCH STREET

Informal street stalls, such as this one in Church Street (ABOVE), offer a delightful selection of bric-à-brac to shoppers, who'll find anything from an old teddy to antique china and silverware. Architectural icons of the turn of the 20th century bring a compelling charm to Long Street (OPPOSITE), one of the oldest streets in Cape Town.

LONG STREET

Les échoppes dans les rues, comme celle-ci dans Church Street (CI-CONTRE), offrent un choix fascinant de bric-à-brac. On y trouve de tout, du vieil ours en peluche aux porcelaines les plus fines. Long Street, une des plus anciennes rue de Cape Town (CI-DESSUS) possède des exemplaires typiques de l'architecture du début du 20ème siècle.

Einfache Straßenstände, wie etwa dieser in der Church Street (GEGENÜBER), bieten eine wunderbare Auswahl an Nippes und Antiquitäten. Besucher stöbern zwischen alten Teddybären, Porzellan und Silber herum. Die schmucken Gebäude der Jahrhundertwende verleihen der Long Street, eine der ältesten Straßen von Kapstadt, große Anziehungskraft (OBEN).

BO-KAAP ARCHITECTURE

Restored houses dating back to the late 18th century (ABOVE) bring splashes of colour to the quiet cobbled streets and tidy avenues of the Malay Quarter, or Bo-Kaap, on the lower slopes of Signal Hill, just a short motorbike ride (OPPOSITE) from the city centre. The Bo-Kaap is home to a large Islamic community whose ancestors came to South Africa as slaves from Java, Bali, Timor, Celibes and former Ceylon.

MALAY QUARTER VIGNETTE

Ces maisons restaurées de la fin du 18ième aux couleurs vives (CI-CONTRE) égayent les ruelles et avenues tranquilles du Malay Quarter, ou Bo-Kaap, sur Signal Hill, près du centre ville (CI-DESSUS). Le Bo-Kaap est le quartier où réside une importante communauté Islamique, descendante des esclaves importés autrefois de Java, Bali, Timor, Célèbes et Ceylan.

Restaurierte Häuser aus dem späten 18. Jahrhundert (GEGENÜBER) bringen Farbenfreudigkeit in die Kopfsteinpflastergassen in Kapstadts Malaienviertel, oder Bo-Kaap, das an den unteren Hängen des Signalhügels liegt. Mit dem Motorrad (OBEN) ist man schnell im Stadtzentrum. In diesem Viertel lebt eine große muslimische Gemeinschaft, deren Vorfahren als Sklaven aus Java, Bali, Timor und dem ehemaligen Ceylon stammen.

COBRA RIDE, RATANGA JUNCTION

CROCODILE GORGE RIVER RIDE

Two of the fun rides at Ratanga Junction, Africa's biggest theme park, which is situated on the outskirts of Cape Town.

Deux des attractions principales de Ratanga Junction, le plus grand parc de loisirs d'Afrique, situé aux abords de Cape Town.

Nervenkitzel und Spaß bieten die Fahrten in Ratanga Junction, dem größten Vergnügungspark in Afrika, der am Stadtrand von Kapstadt liegt.

SIDEWALK BARBER

This alfresco barber's shop in Nyanga on the Cape Flats offers the latest coiffures (ABOVE). An informal trader displays her colourful wares (OPPOSITE) on the ground at the Khayelitsha taxi rank, which is an important concourse for hundreds of thousands of commuters into and out of Cape Town.

TAXI RANK TRADER

Ce figaro de Nyanga, aux Cape Flats, offre le dernier cri en coiffure dans son salon en plein air (CI-CONTRE). Une marchande de rue étale ses marchandises bariolées (CI-DESSUS) à une station de taxis, où passent des centaines de milliers de navetteurs se rendant à Cape Town.

Dieser Freiluft-Friseur, der sein Geschäft in Nyanga, einem Wohngebiet in den Cape Flats, betreibt, bietet seiner Kundschaft die neuesten Trends in der Haarmode (GEGENÜBER). An einem Taxenstand breitet eine Straßenhändlerin ihre farbenfreudigen Artikel auf der Erde zum Verkauf aus (OBEN), denn dies ist ein wichtiger Knotenpunkt für hunderttausende Pendler auf dem Weg von und nach Kapstadt.

CLIFTON AND THE TWELVE APOSTLES

With the imposing presence of the Twelve Apostles in the background, Atlantic breakers sweep across the idyllic sands of Clifton's four beaches (ABOVE) which, together with nearby Camps Bay beach (OPPOSITE), are major drawcards for summer holiday-makers from all over the world.

CAMPS BAY

Dominés par les 'Twelve Apostles', les brisants de l'Atlantique déferlent sur les plages idylliques de Clifton (CI-CONTRE), qui, avec Camps Bay (CI-DESSUS), attirent les vacanciers du monde entier.

Im Hintergrund ragt die eindrucksvolle Gebirgskette der Zwölf Apostel auf, und vorne spülen die Brecher des Atlantik über die vier schönen Sandstrände von Clifton (GEGENÜBER). Zusammen mit dem nahegelegenen Strand von Camps Bay (OBEN), bilden sie die beliebtesten Attraktionen für die Sommerurlauber aus aller Welt.

KIRSTENBOSCH RESTAURANT

Kirstenbosch National Botanical Garden is a sanctuary for 4,700 species of flora, nearly 50 per cent of the Peninsula's floral kingdom.

Le jardin botanique de Kirstenbosch où sont préservées 4,700 espèces de plantes, près de la moitié de toutes les variétés trouvées dans la Péninsule.

Der Nationale Botanische Garten von Kirstenbosch ist ein Schutzgebiet für 4,700 Pflanzenarten, nahezu fünfzig Prozent des Pflanzenreiches der Halbinsel.

KIRSTENBOSCH KALEIDOSCOPE

GROOT CONSTANTIA

HARVESTING GRAPES, GROOT CONSTANTIA

Cape Dutch homesteads, such as the one at Groot Constantia, nestle among the oaks and vineyards of the south-western Cape's wine farms.

———————

Groot Constantia, ainsi que bien d'autres demeures anciennes en style hollandais du Cap, est niché entre les chênes et les vignobles de la région.

———————

Auf den Weingütern am Kap, eingebettet zwischen Eichen und Weinbergen, stehen Häuser im kap-holländischen Stil, wie das Herrenhaus in Groot Constantia.

HOUT BAY HARBOUR

The air hangs heavy with the scent of freshly caught snoek, and seagulls hover for the spoils as boats bring their harvest ashore at Hout Bay Harbour (ABOVE), popular for its cruises to the seal colony at Duiker Island nearby. A seaside eatery on the fringes of the bay beneath Chapman's Peak (OPPOSITE) offers visitors 'the best fish and chips south of the Equator'.

FISH ON THE ROCKS, HOUT BAY

L'odeur de poisson frais flotte dans l'air, et les mouettes suivent de près les chalutiers retournant au port de Hout Bay (CI-CONTRE) avec leur pêche. Hout Bay est populaire pour les excursions aux colonies de phoques de Duiker Island. Un petit restaurant aux abords de la baie, au pied de Chapman's Peak, (CI-DESSUS) offre 'le meilleur poisson frit avec frites, au sud de l'équateur'.

Der Geruch frisch gefangener Fische hängt in der Luft, und die Möwen kreisen über den Booten, die ihre Ladung in den Hafen von Hout Bay einbringen (GEGENÜBER). Von hier aus werden auch Kreuzfahrten zu den Robbenkolonien auf der nahe gelegenen Duiker-Insel angeboten. Am Rande der Bucht, unterhalb des Chapman's Peak, liegt ein Fischlokal (OBEN), das 'den besten Fisch mit Pommes südlich des Äquators' anpreist.

Holiday-makers flock to the sweeping beaches of the False Bay coastline in summer, to revel in the water that is considerably warmer than on the western side of the peninsula, or to experience the delights of Muizenberg's entertainment complex (RIGHT), which includes a pavilion, a children's amusement park and a cluster of swimming pools.

En été, les vacanciers envahissent les longues plages du littoral de False Bay, pour se prélasser dans les eaux plus chaudes de ce côté de la péninsule, ou encore, visiter le parc d'attractions de Muizenberg (À DROITE). On y trouve un pavillon, des attractions spéciales pour enfants et plusieurs piscines.

In den Sommermonaten kommen Scharen von Feriengästen an die ausladenden Strände der False Bay (Falsche Bucht), um die Badefreuden in dem warmen Wasser zu genießen oder sich in dem Unterhaltungskomplex von Muizenberg (Bildmitte) zu amüsieren (RECHTS). Hier gibt es einen Pavillon, verschiedene Schwimmbecken und Anlagen für Kinder.

MUIZENBERG'S SUNSHINE COAST

BOULDERS BEACH

Boulders beach near Simon's Town, one of only two mainland colonies of African Jackass penguins, is a haven for bathers and bird-lovers.

Boulder's Beach, à Simon's Town, est un paradis pour baigneurs et ornithologues; on y trouve l'une des deux seules colonies de manchots du continent.

Boulders Beach, wo sich eine der nur zwei Kolonien der bedrohten Brillenpenguine auf dem Festland befindet, erfreut Badelustige und Vogelliebhaber.

BATHING BOOTHS, ST JAMES

St James' bathing booths (ABOVE) are perfectly reflected in the unruffled waters of this small tidal pool. Nearby Fish Hoek beach (OPPOSITE), one of the Cape Peninsula's most popular bathing beaches, is a mecca for sun-seekers and a venue for hobie-cat regattas and other watersports. The clear, warm water offers safe swimming and surfing, and snorkellers have the chance to explore the submarine beauty of the kelp forests.

FISH HOEK BEACH

Les cabines de bains à St James (CI-CONTRE) se reflètent à la perfection dans les eaux calmes de cette petite lagune. Toute proche, la plage de Fish Hoek (CI-DESSUS) est la Mecque des fanatiques du bronzage. Les régates de catamarans et autres sports aquatiques y sont populaires, et ses eaux limpides et chaudes sont idéales pour la nage et le surfing. Les plongeurs pourront y explorer les merveilles des forêts sous-marines de laminaires.

In der kleinen Lagune widerspiegeln sich die Badekabinen bei St. James (GEGENÜBER). Der nahe gelegene Strand von Fish Hoek (OBEN) ist einer der beliebtesten der Kap-Halbinsel – ein Paradies für Sonnenhungrige, wo auch Regatten ausgetragen und andere Wassersportarten betrieben werden. Das klare Wasser ist ideal zum Schwimmen und Wellenreiten und man kann die schöne Unterwasserwelt der Seetangwälder erkunden.

CAPE OF GOOD HOPE NATURE RESERVE

Fynbos-covered folds of granite form the peninsula that snakes towards Cape Point (ABOVE). A lighthouse (OPPOSITE) warns seafarers of treacherous seas.

La péninsule (CI-DESSUS), où foisonne une végétation unique, serpente vers Cape Point. Un phare (CI-CONTRE) guide les marins dans les eaux traîtresses.

Bewachsene Granithügel bilden die Halbinsel, die sich bis zur Kapspitze erstreckt (OBEN). Ein Leuchtturm (GEGENÜBER) warnt vor gefährlichen Gewässern.

CAPE POINT LIGHTHOUSE

DORP STREET, STELLENBOSCH

Historical homesteads line Dorp Street (ABOVE) in Stellenbosch. A landmark is Oom Samie se Winkel (OPPOSITE), a general dealer's store.

Les demeures historiques dans Dorp Street à Stellenbosch (CI-DESSUS). Oom Samie se Winkel (CI-CONTRE) est un bazar renommé de l'endroit.

Historische Häuser säumen die Dorp Street (Dorfstraße) in Stellenbosch (OBEN). Oom Samie se Winkel (GEGENÜBER) ist ein alter Kolonialwarenladen.

OOM SAMIE SE WINKEL

BOSCHENDAL

LANZERAC

The manor house of Boschendal (OPPOSITE) which, like Lanzerac (ABOVE), reflects the architecture brought to the Cape by Dutch settlers centuries ago.

———

Les manoirs de Boschendal (CI-CONTRE) et de Lanzerac (CI-DESSUS) sont des exemples typiques de l'architecture introduite autrefois par les colons hollandais.

———

Die Herrenhäuser auf Boschendal (GEGENÜBER) und Lanzerac (OBEN) reflektieren den Baustil, den holländische Siedler vor Jahrhunderten am Kap einführten.

the winelands

46

STRAWBERRY FARM

Deep blue skies and distant mountains form a stunning backdrop to this colourful montage of farm life at Mooiberge Strawberry Farmstall near Stellenbosch (ABOVE). Farmstalls such as this, which sell their wares at the roadside throughout the winelands (OPPOSITE), showcase an abundant harvest of vegetables and succulent fruits.

ROADSIDE FARMSTALL

Le ciel d'azur et les montagnes créent un magnifique décor pour ce montage bariolé (CI-CONTRE), représentant une scène à la ferme de Mooi-berge près de Stellenbosch. Nombreuses sont les fermes (CI-DESSUS) qui, comme celle-ci, vendent leurs abondantes récoltes de succulents fruits et légumes, au bord des nombreuses routes qui sillonnent les vignobles.

Strahlend blauer Himmel und die Bergketten am Horizont bilden eine großartige Kulisse für diesen farbenfreudigen Aufbau vom Landleben bei dem Verkaufsstand der Mooiberge Erdbeerfarm in der Nähe von Stellen-bosch (GEGENÜBER). Verkaufsstände, wie dieser, die ihre Erzeugnisse am Straßenrand anbieten, gibt es im ganzen Weinland (OBEN), und sie veran-schaulichen die reichhaltige Ernte an Gemüse und saftigem Obst.

GATHERING WATERBLOMMETJIES

LA BRI ESTATE

Snow-capped mountain giants tower above the fertile valleys of La Bri Wine Estate (LEFT) near Paarl, while farm workers (OPPOSITE) in the winelands wade waist-deep in water to pluck a delicious harvest of Cape Pondweed, used in a traditional Afrikaans dish known as *waterblommetjiebredie*.

Ces hautes montagnes aux sommets enneigés, surplombent les vallées fertiles du domaine vinicole de La Bri (À GAUCHE), près de Paarl. Ces paysans (CI-CONTRE), dans l'eau jusqu'à la taille, récoltent des délicieux potamots du Cap qui sont utilisés dans la préparation du 'waterblommetjiebredie', un ragoût traditionnel afrikaans.

Schneebedeckte Berggipfel ragen hinter den fruchtbaren Tälern des La Bri Weingutes (LINKS) bei Paarl empor, während Landarbeiter (GEGENÜBER) bis zur Hüfte im Wasser stehen, um das delikate Laichkraut zu ernten, das für ein einheimisches Gericht, Waterblommetjiebredie, verwendet wird.

HEX RIVER VALLEY

The vineyards of the Hex River Valley (ABOVE) hang heavy with a variety of cultivars, some of them destined for Franschhoek's Cabrière Estate (OPPOSITE).

La Hex River Valley (CI-DESSUS) produit une variété de cultivars, dont certains sont destinés au domaine de la Cabrière à Franschhoek (CI-CONTRE).

Weinfelder im Tal des Hexenflusses (OBEN). Von den vielen Rebsorten sind einige für das Weingut Clos Cabrière bei Franschhoek (GEGENÜBER) bestimmt.

CABRIÈRE CELLARS, FRANSCHHOEK

WHALE-WATCHERS, HERMANUS

Southern right whales carouse and cruise with their newborn calves off the rocky shoreline of Hermanus (ABOVE) between July and December, attracting thousands of whale-watchers to the nutrient-rich waters of the Cape coast. Taking advantage of the numbers, a whale crier (OPPOSITE) announces the best places to see these gentle leviathans at play.

WHALE CRIER

Entre juillet et décembre, des milliers de touristes viennent à Hermanus pour voir les baleines et leurs nouveau-nés s'ébattre dans les vagues, proche de la côte rocheuse (CI-CONTRE). Un crieur public (CI-DESSUS) informe les nombreux visiteurs des meilleurs endroits pour observer les géants des mers.

Südliche Glattwale tummeln sich von Juli bis Dezember mit ihren Jungen vor der felsigen Küste bei Hermanus (GEGENÜBER) und locken Tausende von Walbeobachtern an die Kapküste. Der 'Wal-Verkünder' (OBEN) gibt Auskunft, an welcher Stelle in der Walker-Bucht sich die sanften Meeresriesen gerade aufhalten.

FISHING OFF ARNISTON

Fishermen in flimsy craft lower their lines long and deep off the rugged coast of Arniston (ABOVE), a haven for writers, poets and others seeking refuge from the rat race. The salt-encrusted walls of this old fishing cottage (OPPOSITE) at Arniston (which is also known as Waenhuiskrans) have lost their fight against the sea and sun, but they're home to a seafarer and his family, who live off the fruits of his daily catches.

FISHERMAN'S COTTAGE, ARNISTON

Des pêcheurs dans leurs petites embarcations, laissent tomber leurs lignes au large d'Arniston (CI-CONTRE). L'endroit est recherché pour le calme qu'il offre, et nombreux sont les écrivains, poètes et artistes qui s'y sont installés. Cette vieille masure (CI-DESSUS) à Arniston (Waenhuiskrans), aux murs encroûtés de sel, a perdu la bataille contre les éléments, mais pour le marin et sa famille qui vivent des produits de la mer, c'est leur home.

Vor der felsigen Küste bei Arniston lassen Fischer in kleinen Booten ihre Leinen ins Meer gleiten (GEGENÜBER). Der Ort ist eine Zuflucht für Schriftsteller, Dichter und andere, die der Hektik entfliehen wollen. Die salzverkrusteten Mauern dieser alten Fischerkate (OBEN) in Arniston (auch bekannt als Waenhuiskrans) haben den Kampf gegen See und Sonne verloren, aber für den Fischer und seine Familie sind sie das Zuhause.

WOLFBERG ARCH, CEDARBERG

MALTESE CROSS

The rocky heights of the Cedarberg mountains have been eroded over aeons to form a geological wonderland of bizarre sandstone formations.

Les hauteurs rocailleuses des montagnes du Cedarberg ont été érodées au cours de milliards d'années, créant ainsi un paysage surnaturel.

Die Felsenlandschaft der Zederberge verwitterte über Jahrmillionen und es entstand eine geologische Wunderwelt aus bizarren Sandsteinformationen.

LAMBERT'S BAY

A thriving fleet of gaily coloured fishing boats trawls the pelagic waters off Lambert's Bay (ABOVE), along the West Coast north of Cape Town. The fish-rich waters of the Atlantic Ocean also attract about 5,000 pairs of Cape gannets (OPPOSITE), which compete for roosting space on Bird Island in spring and summer.

CAPE GANNETS, LAMBERT'S BAY

Une flottille de chalutiers aux couleurs vives pêche dans les eaux au large de Lambert's Bay (CI-CONTRE), sur la côte Ouest, au nord de Cape Town. L'Atlantique aux eaux abondantes en poisson, attire également quelque 5,000 couples de fous de Bassan (CI-DESSUS) qui viennent nicher sur l'île de Bird Island au printemps et en été.

Eine beachtliche Flotte von bunten Fischerbooten fischt mit Schleppnetzen in den Gewässern vor Lambert's Bay (GEGENÜBER) an der Westküste, nördlich von Kapstadt. Die reichen Fischgründe des Atlantik locken auch die etwa 5,000 Paare von Kaptölpeln an (OBEN), die sich im Frühling und Sommer auf der Vogelinsel um Nistplätze drängeln.

NAMAQUALAND DAISIES

LANGEBAAN SPLENDOUR

Late winter rains transform the arid coastline near Langebaan into a springtime wonderland, carpeting the countryside with Namaqualand daisies.

Les dernières pluies hivernales métamorphosent la côte aride de Langebaan en un eldorado printanier, tapissant le paysage de pâquerettes du Namaqualand.

Später Winterregen verwandelt den trockenen Küstenstreifen bei Langebaan in einen Frühlingstraum mit Blütenteppichen von Margeriten.

ST HELENA BAY

The West Coast is typified by the rustic beauty of a dirt road and a lazy sea (ABOVE). Near Springbok a donkey cart transports rural folk (OPPOSITE).

Un tableau rustique, typique de la côte Ouest (CI-DESSUS). Près de Springbok, un couple de paysans passe dans leur carriole tirée par des ânes (CI-CONTRE).

Die rustikale Schönheit der Westküste: Sandstraße und Meer (OBEN). Eine Eselkarre befördert Landbewohner bei Springbok (GEGENÜBER).

GOEGAP NATURE RESERVE

CANOEING IN THE RICHTERSVELD

Cracked and folded by seismic forces millions of years ago, the Richtersveld mountains (LEFT) give way to a gentler landscape of rivers and rolling hills near Loeriesfontein in the Northern Cape. This area is home to the quiver tree (OPPOSITE), so named because its bark was used by the San to make quivers for their poisoned arrows.

QUIVER TREES

Crevassées et plissées par d'anciennes forces séismiques, les montagnes du Richtersveld (CI-CONTRE) se transforment en un paisible paysage vallonné et arrosé de rivières, près de Loeriesfontein, dans le Northern Cape. Cette région abrite le 'quiver tree', (arbre-carquois) (CI-DESSUS), ainsi nommé parce que les San façonnaient les carquois pour leurs flèches empoisonnées avec son écorce.

Gewaltige Erdbeben vor Jahrmillionen verursachten die Spaltungen und Falten der Richtersveld-Berge (GEGENÜBER), die dann bei Loeriesfontein im Nord-Kapland in eine lieblichere Landschaft mit Flußbetten und sanften Hügeln übergehen. Hier wächst der Köcherbaum (OBEN), so benannt, weil die San daraus Köcher für ihre Giftpfeile anfertigten.

augrabies falls

66

Roaring like some angry river god, a seething cauldron of white water plunges into an abyss at Bridal Veil Falls, Augrabies (RIGHT), in the Northern Cape, on its journey to the sea at Alexander Bay. The ochre dunes and dry river beds of the Kgalagadi Transfrontier Park (formerly the Kalahari Gemsbok National Park) are the perfect environment for the gemsbok (OPPOSITE), which has adapted to survive its hostile environment without water for months.

BRIDAL VEIL FALLS, AUGRABIES

KGALAGADI TRANSFRONTIER PARK

Bouillonnante de colère, la rivière plonge dans l'abysse de Bridal Veil Falls à Augrabies dans le Northern Cape (CI-CONTRE), en route vers Alexander Bay, où elle se jettera dans la mer. Les dunes ocres et les lits de rivières à sec du Kgalagadi Transfrontier Park (anciennement le Kalahari Gemsbok National Park) sont l'habitat idéal pour le gemsbok (CI-DESSUS) qui s'est adapté aux conditions hostiles et sait survivre des mois sans boire.

Tosend ergießen sich die Wassermassen in den Abgrund und bilden die Bridal Veil Falls, Augrabies (GEGENÜBER), im Nord-Kapland ehe sie weiterfließen bis zum Meer bei Alexander Bay. In den Dünen und trockenen Flußbetten im Kgalagadi Transfrontier Park (Kalahari Gemsbok Nationalpark) leben Oryxantilopen (OBEN), die sich den harten Bedingungen dieser Welt angepaßt haben und monatelang ohne Wasser überleben können.

COUNTRY BREADBASKET

Bathed in the sunlight of late afternoon, a farmstead stands like an island amid the rolling green wheatlands of the Overberg (ABOVE). The area is so rich in grains that it is known as the 'breadbasket of South Africa'. A yellow eiderdown of canolas carpets the gentle undulations of the countryside near Swellendam (OPPOSITE).

CANOLA FIELDS, SWELLENDAM

Baignée par la lumière du crépuscule, une ferme semble flotter comme une île dans l'océan de verdure que sont les champs de blé dans l'Over-berg (CI-CONTRE). La région est tellement fertile en céréales qu'on l'appelle 'le grenier de l'Afrique du Sud'. Le tapis jaune des champs de colza recouvre les ondulations du paysage près de Swellendam (CI-DESSUS).

In das warme Sonnenlicht am Spätnachmittag getaucht, nimmt sich ein Bauernhaus wie eine Insel aus in den wogenden Weizenfeldern des Overberg (GEGENÜBER). Dies ist gutes Getreidegebiet und bekannt als 'die Kornkammer Südafrikas'. Die Rapsfelder wirken wie eine gelbe Stepp-decke auf der sanft geschwungenen Landschaft bei Swellendam (OBEN).

ostrich country

OSTRICH COUNTRY, DE RUST

Known as the domain of the ostrich barons, the scrublands of the Little Karoo near Oudtshoorn and De Rust (ABOVE) are an ideal environment for these large birds, renowned for their export feathers and fleetness of foot. Nearby, beneath the Swartberg Mountain Range, are the Cango Caves (OPPOSITE), a geologic wonderland of beautiful and bizarre limestone formations which attract thousands to its subterranean chambers every year.

THE CANGO CAVES

Domaine des barons de l'autruche, le terrain broussailleux du Little Karoo près d'Oudtshoorn et De Rust (CI-CONTRE), est l'environnement idéal pour ces énormes oiseaux, renommés pour leur plumage et la vitesse à laquelle savent les transporter leurs pattes agiles. Près de là, au pied de la chaîne du Swartberg, les Cango Caves (CI-DESSUS) attirent annuellement des milliers de visiteurs qui viennent admirer ses étranges formations calcaires.

Für Strauße ist die Buschsteppe in der Kleinen Karoo bei Oudtshoorn und De Rust (GEGENÜBER) ein idealer Lebensraum. In dieser Gegend der 'Federbarone' ist der schnelle Landvogel mit den schönen Federn ein wichtiger Bewohner. Ganz in der Nähe, unterhalb der Swartbergkette, liegen die Cango-Höhlen (OBEN), eine geologische Märchenwelt aus wundersamen, bizarren Kalksteinformationen in unterirdischen Sälen.

WILDERNESS WONDERLAND

Washed by the gentle breakers of the Indian Ocean, copper sands curl
around the coast at Wilderness (ABOVE), a tranquil seaside retreat for nature
lovers looking for quietude, long walks on the beach and lazy days in the sun.
Further east, at Knysna (OPPOSITE), the sea breaks through the mainland at
The Heads to form a gracious tidal lagoon at the town's feet.

KNYSNA LAGOON

Le ressac paisible de l'océan Indien baigne les sables d'or du littoral à Wilderness (CI-CONTRE), un petit village tranquille où se retrouvent ceux qui recherchent le calme, et aiment les longues promenades sur la plage. Plus à l'est, à Knysna (CI-DESSUS), la mer pénètre dans l'intérieur par les 'Heads', formant un charmant lagon en bordure même de la ville.

Umspült von den sanft auslaufenden Wellen des Indischen Ozeans und umrandet von kupferfarbenen Stränden, bietet die Küste bei Wilderness (GEGENÜBER) einen beschaulichen Erholungsort für Naturfreunde, die geruhsame Sonnentage und lange Strandspaziergänge genießen. Weiter östlich, bei Knysna (OBEN), strömt das Meer zwischen den beiden Land-zungen, The Heads, hindurch und bildet eine malerische Gezeitenlagune.

garden route

74

PLETTENBERG BAY

Plettenberg Bay's Beacon Isle Hotel (ABOVE) stands in five-star splendour on the water's edge, its rooms and restaurants facing the sea. At Christmas time 'Plet' is a teeming melting pot of tourists who flock to its popular bathing beaches. The more rustically inclined prefer the deep rainforests and seaside seclusion of Storms River in the Tsitsikamma National Park, spanned by a suspension bridge at its mouth (OPPOSITE).

STORMS RIVER MOUTH

Le Beacon Isle Hotel à Plettenberg Bay domine la plage de toute sa splendeur (CI-CONTRE), ses chambres et restaurants donnant sur la mer. A l'époque de Noël, 'Plet' devient un melting-pot regorgeant de touristes affluant sur ses plages très en vogue. D'autres, préférant le calme, iront à la découverte dans les forêts subtropicales, et apprécieront l'isolement de la Storms River dans le Tsitsikamma National Park (CI-DESSUS).

Beacon Isle Hotel (GEGENÜBER) bei Plettenberg Bay bietet Fünf-Sterne-Luxus: Restaurants und Zimmer mit Meerblick. Zur Weihnachtszeit ist Hochbetrieb in 'Plet'. Besucher aus aller Welt bevölkern die Badestrände. Andere ziehen die tiefen Wälder und abgelegenen Küstengebiete und die Flußlandschaft des Storms River im Tsitsikamma Nationalpark vor. An der Flußmündung spannt sich eine Hängebrücke über das Wasser (OBEN).

little karoo

76

MORAVIAN CHURCH, AMALIENSTEIN

The Moravian Church at Amalienstein (LEFT) reflects the humble beginnings of the town which started as a mission station for the small, rustic community there. Simplicity prevails at Haarlem, a tiny Karoo village where many travel by donkey cart (OPPOSITE).

Le temple morave à Amalienstein (À GAUCHE) témoigne des humbles origines de la ville qui, au début, n'était qu'une modeste mission desservant une petite communauté de paysans. La simplicité est de rigueur à Haarlem, un petit hameau du Karoo où la carriole est le moyen de transport principal (CI-CONTRE).

Die Herrenhuter Brüderkirche in Amalienstein (LINKS) deutet auf die bescheidenen Anfänge des Dorfes, das als Missionsstation für die kleine Landbevölkerung begann. Schlichtheit kennzeichnet auch Haarlem, ein kleines Karoodorf, wo die Eselkarre noch viel benutztes Transportmittel ist (GEGENÜBER).

HAARLEM TRANSPORT

DE HEL

OUDTSHOORN ALOES

A tortuous dirt track leads to the tiny settlement of De Hel (OPPOSITE). Stands of aloes (ABOVE) bring splashes of colour to the arid Little Karoo.

Une piste rocailleuse serpente vers le minuscule village de De Hel (CI-CONTRE). Un groupe d'aloès (CI-DESSUS) colore le paysage aride du Little Karoo.

Ein beschwerlicher Pfad führt zu dem winzigen Dorf, De Hel (GEGENÜBER). Aloengruppen (OBEN) bringen Farbtupfer in die öde Landschaft der Kleinen Karoo.

port elizabeth & environs

80

KING'S BEACH, PORT ELIZABETH

Cool surf and scorching summers bring the crowds flocking to Port Elizabeth's King's Beach (ABOVE), a popular bathing and surfing spot, and also a regular venue for hobie-cat regattas. Rhinos are one of the main attractions at Shamwari Game Reserve (OPPOSITE), the only sanctuary in the Eastern Cape which is home to the prized Big Five. Privately owned Shamwari is renowned for its sumptuous, colonial-style accommodation.

SHAMWARI GAME RESERVE

Durant les chaleurs caniculaires de l'été, les vagues rafraîchissantes de King's Beach, à Port Elizabeth (CI-CONTRE) attirent les baigneurs, les surfeurs et les amateurs de régates en grands nombres. Les rhinos sont une des grosses attractions à Shamwari Game Reserve (CI-DESSUS), renommée pour le luxe de son ancien style colonial. Shamwari est la seule réserve de la province où l'on trouve les 5 grands fauves d'Afrique.

Erfrischendes Wasser und heiße Sommertage locken die Scharen nach King's Beach in Port Elizabeth (GEGENÜBER), ein beliebter Strand zum Baden und Wellenreiten und für Regatten. Nashörner sind eine große Attraktion im Shamwari Wildpark (OBEN), dem einzigen Wildschutzgebiet am Ostkap, wo man die Großen Fünf sehen kann. Shamwari ist Privatbesitz und bekannt für seine luxuriösen Unterkünfte im Kolonialstil.

great karoo

VALLEY OF DESOLATION, NEAR GRAAFF-REINET

ADDO ELEPHANT NATIONAL PARK

Jagged rocks loom above the Valley of Desolation near Graaff-Reinet (OPPOSITE). An African elephant drinks at Addo Park, near Port Elizabeth (ABOVE).

Ces roches déchiquetées gardent la Valley of Desolation (CI-CONTRE), près de Graaff-Reinet. Un éléphant se désaltère à Addo Elephant Park (CI-DESSUS).

Die schroffen Felsvorsprünge ragen hinaus über das Tal der Einöde (GEGENÜBER). Ein afrikanischer Elefant beim Trinken im Addo Elephant Nationalpark (OBEN).

grahamstown

84

Exotic garments from distant lands are peddled by a flamboyant trader at a colourful craft market in the university city of Grahamstown (RIGHT). The informality of the stalls contrasts with ornate yet rigid façades of buildings in the centre of the city (OPPOSITE), many of which date back to the early 19th century, when Grahamstown served as a garrison for British forces.

CRAFT MARKET TRADER

COLONIAL CULTURE

Au pittoresque marché de la ville universitaire de Grahamstown (CI-CONTRE), un marchand exubérant colporte des vêtements exotiques venant de pays lointains. Les éventaires plutôt désordonnés contrastent avec les façades ornementées, bien qu'austères, des immeubles du centre ville (CI-DESSUS), dont un nombre remontent au début du 19ième, à l'époque où Grahamstown était une ville de garnison pour les forces britanniques.

Exotische Kleidungsstücke aus fernen Ländern bietet ein lustiger Händler auf dem farbenfreudigen Handarbeitsmarkt der Universitätsstadt Grahamstown an (GEGENÜBER). Die einfachen Stände bilden einen Kontrast zu den steifen Fassaden der Gebäude im Stadtzentrum (OBEN), von denen viele aus dem frühen 19. Jahrhundert stammen, als Grahamstown eine Garnisonsstadt der britischen Truppen war.

XHOSA INITIATES, NEAR CATHCART

Xhosa boys undergoing the transition to manhood (ABOVE). The Hogsback highlands reverberate with the songs of a young herder (OPPOSITE).

Adolescents Xhosa suivant les rites de passage à l'âge adulte (CI-DESSUS). Le Hogsback résonne du chant d'un jeune gardien de troupeau (CI-CONTRE).

Xhosajungen während der Mannbarkeitsriten (OBEN). Musik und Gesang eines Hirtenbuben erfüllen die Luft im Hochland des Hogsback (GEGENÜBER).

COWHERD, HOGSBACK

XHOSA WOMAN

Gentle hills and valleys, dotted with rustic thatched huts, criss-cross the interior of the Eastern Cape (ABOVE), where Xhosa women eke out a modest living from the soil. At the Wild Coast, erosion by wind, water and sand has sculpted geological masterpieces in rock like this one at Hole-in-the-Wall (OPPOSITE), near Coffee Bay.

HOLE-IN-THE-WALL

L'Eastern Cape est une région de vallons tranquilles, éparpillés de huttes au toit de chaume (CI-CONTRE), et où les femmes Xhosa s'échinent à cultiver le sol. Sur la Wild Coast des chefs-d'œuvre géologiques comme le 'Hole-in-the-Wall' près de Coffee Bay (CI-DESSUS), ont été sculptés dans les rochers par le vent, l'océan et le sable.

Sanfte Hügel und Täler mit verstreuten, strohgedeckten Hütten erstrecken sich über das Inland des Ostkaps (GEGENÜBER), wo Xhosafrauen dem kargen Boden einen bescheidenen Lebensunterhalt abringen. An der Wildküste haben Wind und Wasser geologische Meisterwerke geschaffen, wie dieses 'Loch-in-der-Wand' (OBEN) bei Coffee Bay.

durban

90

DURBAN HARBOUR

The concrete monoliths along Durban's Esplanade rise above serried ranks
of yachts (ABOVE) as dawn breaks across the harbour in a blaze of crimson
hues. Swells advance towards the bronze sands of the city's Golden Mile
(OPPOSITE), inviting surfers and swimmers to test their gentle curves. Luxury
hotels line Durban's subtropical beaches and offer stunning views across the
expanse of the Indian Ocean.

THE GOLDEN MILE

Baignés dans la lumière pourpre de l'aube, ces monolithes de béton sur l'Esplanade à Durban, dominent les yachts amarrés en rangs serrés (CI-CONTRE). La houle déferle paisiblement sur les sables dorés du Golden Mile (CI-DESSUS), invitant les surfeurs et baigneurs. Les hôtels de grand luxe bordent les plages subtropicales de Durban, leurs chambres offrant une vue splendide sur l'immensité de l'océan Indien.

Im Licht der Morgendämmerung ragen die Betonsäulen der Hochhäuser an der Esplanade von Durban hinter den Masten der Jachten im Hafen empor (GEGENÜBER). Die auslaufende Dünung vor dem Sandstrand an der 'Goldenen Meile' (OBEN) lockt Wellenreiter und Schwimmer. Luxushotels an den subtropischen Stränden von Durban bieten atemberaubende Aussichten über die endlose Weite des Indischen Ozeans.

ESPLANADE CRAFTS

RICKSHA RIDES

Durban Esplanade is a riot of vibrant colours produced by a huge array of African crafts (OPPOSITE) and the lavish headgear of ricksha drivers (LEFT), who thrill their passengers with bucking-bronco rides up and down the beachfront promenades.

L'Esplanade de Durban est une pro-fusion de couleurs venant de l'énorme gamme de produits d'artisanat africain (CI-CONTRE) et des coiffes somptueuses des conducteurs de ricksha (À GAUCHE). Ceux-ci amusent leurs passagers en leur donnant un parcours mouvementé sur la promenade le long de la plage.

Die Esplanade in Durban ist ein Kaleidoskop von leuchtenden Farben durch die vielen afrikanischen Handar-beiten (GEGENÜBER) und den pompösen Kopfschmuck der Rikschafahrer (LINKS), die ihre Fahrgäste durch Luftsprünge begeistern, während sie an der Strand-promenade entlang ziehen.

93

HOLIDAY MAGIC

A water wonderland and amusement park (ABOVE) on the doorstep of the Indian Ocean are irresistible attractions to the younger set visiting Durban beachfront. uShaka Sea World (OPPOSITE) is one of the five largest aquariums in the world and has a 1,200-seater dolphin stadium, the largest dolphinarium in Africa.

USHAKA SEA WORLD

Avec ses nombreux jeux aquatiques, ce parc de loisirs (CI-CONTRE) en bordure de l'océan Indien est irrésistible aux jeunes visiteurs. uShaka Sea World (CI-DESSUS), un des cinq plus grands aquariums du monde. Le delphinarium, avec 1,200 places, est le plus grand d'Afrique.

Vergnügen zu Wasser und zu Lande (GEGENÜBER) an der Schwelle des Indischen Ozeans üben einen unwiderstehlich Reiz aus auf die jugendlichen Besucher in Durban. uShaka Sea World (Wasserwelt) (OBEN) zählt zu den fünf größten Aquarien der Welt und hat ein Delphinarium mit 1,200 Sitplätzen – das größte in Afrika.

INDIAN MARKET

The aromas of the East pervade the stalls of Durban's popular Indian Market (ABOVE), a bustling plaza where shoppers can buy anything from hot curries and spicy foods to jewellery, incense and an assortment of trinkets. The hexagonal interior of a mosque (OPPOSITE) affords worshippers a dignified venue for quiet contemplation and prayer.

MOSQUE INTERIOR

Les riches arômes de l'Orient imprègnent les stands de l'Indian Market à Durban (CI-CONTRE), un centre animé où l'on trouve un choix varié de produits, des currys et autres plats épicés, à la bijouterie, en passant par les encens et quantités de babioles. L'aménagement intérieur en hexagonale de cette mosquée (CI-DESSUS), offre aux fidèles un lieu paisible, approprié au recueillement et à la contemplation.

Die betörenden Düfte des Ostens wabern über den Ständen von Durbans beliebtem Indermarkt (GEGENÜBER), ein quirliger Platz, wo alles erhältlich ist, von scharfen Currygerichten und würzigen Speisen, bis zu Schmuck, Weihrauchstäbchen und Tand. Der sechseckige Innenraum einer Moschee (OBEN) bietet den Besuchern einen besinnlichen Raum für Meditation und stille Gebete.

MARGATE

Indian Ocean breakers roll in to the sun-bronzed beaches of Margate (ABOVE) south of Durban, a stone's throw away from five-star resort hotels and beach cabanas. Once notorious for shark attacks, Margate and similar resorts along the Hibiscus Coast offer safe bathing for thousands of holiday-makers who revel in their warm waters every year. Rustling fields of sugar cane (OPPOSITE) cover the gentle contours of the countryside near Pennington.

SUGAR CANE FIELDS, PENNINGTON

Les brisants s'écrasent au pied des hôtels de grand luxe et des cabines de plage à Margate (CI-CONTRE), au sud de Durban. Comme d'autres stations balnéaires sur la Hibiscus Coast, Margate était autrefois connue pour ses attaques de requins; de nos jours, on peut y nager en toute sécurité. Champs de cannes à sucre dans les collines aux environs de Pennington (CI-DESSUS).

Die Wellen des Indischen Ozeans rollen an die sonnigen Strände von Margate (GEGENÜBER), südlich von Durban, nur einen Katzensprung entfernt von Fünf-Sterne-Hotels und Strandhäusern. Früher berüchtigt für Angriffe durch Haie, bieten Margate und andere Ferienorte an der Hibiskusküste heute gefahrlose Badefreuden. Zuckerrohrfelder (OBEN) ziehen sich über die sanft geschwungene Landschaft bei Pennington.

CITY HALL

The Pietermaritzburg City Hall (ABOVE), with its Westminster chiming clock and carillon of twelve bells, is reputed to be the largest all-brick building in the southern hemisphere. It presides over a park-like town that is more than 160 years old, and which takes pride in monuments to its historic past such as the Victorian bandstand (OPPOSITE) in leafy Alexandra Park.

ALEXANDRA PARK

L'Hôtel de Ville de Pietermaritzburg (CI-CONTRE), avec son horloge style Westminster et son carillon à douze cloches, revendique l'honneur d'être le plus gros édifice construit entièrement en briques de l'hémisphère Sud. Il occupe la place d'honneur dans une ville verdoyante et fleurie, fondée il y a plus de 160 ans, et très fière de ses monuments, tel que ce kiosque victorien à Alexandra Park (CI-DESSUS).

Das Rathaus in Pietermaritzburg (GEGENÜBER), mit der Turmuhr im Westminsterstil und dem Glockenspiel mit zwölf Glocken, ist angeblich das größte Backsteingebäude in der südlichen Halbkugel. Es blickt auf die 160jährige, parkartige Stadt, die stolz ist auf ihre historischen Bauwerke, wie etwa der viktorianische Stand für eine Musikkapelle (OBEN) unter den Bäumen im Alexandra Park.

MIDLANDS MEANDER

A Zulu woman weaving on the Midlands Meander (ABOVE), north of Pietermaritzburg. A flurry of water plummets over the Howick Falls (OPPOSITE).

Une Zouloue faisant du tissage dans le Midlands Meander, au nord de Pietermaritzburg (CI-DESSUS). La rivière plonge aux Howick Falls (CI-CONTRE).

Webende Zulufrau an der 'Midlands Meander' nördlich von Pietermaritzburg (OBEN). Die schäumenden Wassermassen der Howick-Fälle (GEGENÜBER).

HOWICK FALLS

RORKE'S DRIFT MUSEUM

The roar of gunfire and the rattle of spears reverberated across the country-side when a small British garrison repulsed an attack by 600 Zulu *impis* at Rorke's Drift in the Natal Midlands in 1879. A museum commemorates the event (ABOVE), while a laager of 64 life-size bronze wagons (OPPOSITE) commemorates the clash between the 465 Boers and 10,000 Zulus at the Battle of Blood River in 1838.

BLOOD RIVER MONUMENT

Le bruit des fusillades et le cliquetis des lances résonnaient à Rorke's drift, dans les Natal Midlands, où en 1879, une petite garnison britannique repoussa une attaque de 600 impis Zoulous. Un musée commémore l'événement (CI-CONTRE). D'autre part, un laager de 64 chariots de bronze (CI-DESSUS) rappelle l'affrontement de 1838 entre 465 Boers et 10,000 Zoulous à Blood River.

Geschützdonner und das Rasseln von Speeren tönte über das Land, als 1879 eine kleine britische Garnison bei Rorke's Drift im Natal Mittelland den Angriff von 600 Zulu Impis abwehrte. Ein Museum erinnert an diese Schlacht (GEGENÜBER), während eine Wagenburg von 64 lebensgroßen Bronzewagen (OBEN) den Kampf zwischen 465 Buren und 10,000 Zulus bei den Schlacht von Blutrivier ins Gedächtnis ruft.

CATHEDRAL PEAK

DRAKENSBERG MOUNTAINSCAPES

Cathedral Peak (OPPOSITE) is one of the 'Berg's more spectacular peaks. In tranquil valleys, subsistence farmers live in splendid isolation (ABOVE).

Cathedral Peak (CI-CONTRE) est un des sommets des plus spectaculaires du Drakensberg. Les fermiers vivent isolés dans les vallées paisibles (CI-DESSUS).

Cathedral Peak (GEGENÜBER) ist einer der beeindruckendsten Gipfel der Drakensberge. In Tälern malerischer Abgeschiedenheit leben Kleinbauern (OBEN).

drakensberg

108

LAMMERGEIER

The bearded vulture, or lammergeier (*Gypaetus barbatus*), occupies the Drakensberg's high ground (ABOVE), nesting on the cliff faces and between the rocky clefts. For centuries they shared this environment with the nomadic San, a group of hunter-gatherers who left a rich legacy of painting on the walls of caves, like this one at Kamberg (OPPOSITE).

SAN ROCK ART

Le 'vautour barbu' ou lammergeier (*Gypaetus barbatus*) réside dans les hauteurs du Drakensberg (CI-CONTRE), et niche dans les fissures des parois rocheuses. Pendant des siècles il se partageait le même environnement avec les San, un groupe de chasseurs nomades qui y laissa leur riche contribution de peintures rupestres, comme celle-ci à Kamberg (CI-DESSUS).

Der Bartgeier oder Lämmergeier (*Gypaetus barbatus*) herrscht über das Hochgebirge der Drakensberge (GEGENÜBER) und nistet an den Abhängen und zwischen Felsschluchten. Jahrhundertelang teilten sie diese Landschaft mit den San, einem nomadischen Jägervolk, das ein reiches Erbe an Felsmalereien in Höhlen hinterließ, wie in dieser bei Kamberg (OBEN).

drakensberg

110

AMPHITHEATRE

Cloaked in a mantle of virgin snow and reflected in the icy waters of a country dam, the fortress-like flanks of the Amphitheatre reveal the full majesty of the Drakensberg (ABOVE). Visitors to Giant's Castle Game Reserve (OPPOSITE) revel in the chill air and beauty of this mountain wilderness and its many trails.

GIANT'S CASTLE GAME RESERVE

Recouverts sous un manteau de neige, et reflétés dans les eaux glacées d'un étang, comme les murailles d'une forteresse, les énormes versants de l'Amphithéâtre révèlent toute l'ampleur du Drakensberg (CI-CONTRE). Les visiteurs au Giant's Castle Game Reserve (CI-DESSUS) jouissent de l'air pur et de la beauté de la nature dans les montagnes.

In einen Mantel von Neuschnee gehüllt, widerspiegelt sich im eiskalten Wasser des Stausees das Bergmassiv des Amphitheaters und veranschaulicht die gewaltige Majestät der Drakensberge (GEGENÜBER). Die Besucher im Naturschutzgebiet Giant's Castle (Burg der Riesen) genießen auf den vielen Wanderwegen die reine, kalte Luft und die Schönheit dieser Bergwildnis (OBEN).

KOSI BAY FISHERMAN

Observing a time-honoured tradition, a Kosi Bay fisherman relies on an elaborate structure of poles and sticks to snare his supper (ABOVE). Larger, concentric fish traps (OPPOSITE), designed to catch their quarry on the outgoing tide, are common in the fish-rich waters of the Kosi Bay Estuary.

TRADITIONAL FISH TRAPS

Suivant une tradition ancestrale, un pêcheur de Kosi Bay (CI-CONTRE) dépend d'un assemblage compliqué de perches et de mâts pour attraper son dîner. Des grands pièges concentriques (CI-DESSUS) sont conçus pour capturer les poissons à la marée descendante; ils sont très répandus dans les eaux poissonneuses de l'estuaire de Kosi Bay.

Entsprechend der überlieferten Art des Fischfangs, verläßt sich der Fischer in der Kosi-Bay (GEGENÜBER) auf die komplizierten Anlagen von Stangen und Stöcken, um sein Abendessen zu fangen. Größere, konzentrisch angelegte Fischfallen (OBEN), zielen darauf ab, ihre Beute bei rückläufiger Flut zu erwischen. Sie sind in den fischreichen Gewässern der Flußmündung in der Kosi-Bay sehr verbreitet.

SODWANA BAY

The warm waters and sweeping coastline of Sodwana Bay (ABOVE) lure anglers, divers and ski-boat enthusiasts to its shores throughout the year. Running the gauntlet of seabird predators, loggerhead turtle hatchlings (OPPOSITE) scurry across the sand near Sodwana Bay to the safety of the sea.

LOGGERHEAD TURTLE HATCHLINGS

Les eaux chaudes et le vaste littoral de Sodwana Bay (CI-CONTRE) attirent les pêcheurs, les plongeurs et les plaisanciers toute l'année durant. Exposées à la menace des prédateurs ailés, ces petites tortues à écailles (CI-DESSUS) se précipitent à travers la plage vers la sécurité de l'océan, près de Sodwana Bay.

Das warme Meer und die schöne Küste von Sodwana Bay (GEGENÜBER) locken Angler, Taucher und Schnellbootfahrer das ganze Jahr hindurch an. Im Spießrutenlauf unter den kreisenden Raubvögeln der Küste, krabbeln die Schlüpflinge der unechten Karettschildkröte (OBEN) über den Sand bei Sodwana Bay, um den Schutz der See zu erreichen.

PHINDA RESOURCE RESERVE

A lion is the centre of attention as he pads through short grass at Phinda
Resource Reserve (ABOVE). A trio of white rhino takes a siesta among the
acacias at the Hluhluwe-Umfolozi Park (OPPOSITE). The game reserves of
northern KwaZulu-Natal, which are among the best in the world, helped
rescue the white rhino from the brink of extinction.

WHITE RHINO, HLUHLUWE-UMFOLOZI PARK

Un lion en promenade attire toute l'attention à Phinda Resource Reserve (CI-CONTRE). Un trio de rhinos blancs fait la sieste entre les acacias à Hluhluwe-Umfolozi Park (CI-DESSUS). Les réserves naturelles dans le nord du KwaZulu-Natal, qui sont parmi les meilleures du monde, furent instrumentales à sauver l'espèce qui était en voie d'extinction.

Der gemächlich einherschreitende Löwe steht im Mittelpunkt der Aufmerksamkeit im Phinda Resource Reserve Naturschutzgebiet (GEGENÜBER). Breitmaulnashörner halten Mittagsruhe unter den Akazien im Hluhluwe-Umfolozi Wildpark (OBEN). Wildschutzgebiete im nördlichen KwaZulu-Natal zählen zu den besten der Welt und haben wesentlich dazu beigetragen, das Breitmaulnashorn vor dem Aussterben zu bewahren.

SHAKALAND DANCERS

Armed with knobkieries, long sticks and shields, Zulu warriors (ABOVE) prepare to perform a war dance for visitors to Shakaland, a cultural village near Eshowe, which has preserved the rich customs and rituals of the Zulu people since the days of Shaka. Beadwork, being created at Dumazulu (OPPOSITE), is an integral part of the Zulu culture.

BEADWORK, DUMAZULU

Armés de leur knobkierie, long bâton et bouclier, des guerriers Zoulous (CI-CONTRE) se préparent à faire une danse de guerre pour les visiteurs à Shakaland, un village culturel près d'Eshowe, qui a préservé les riches traditions et rituels du peuple Zoulou depuis l'ère de Shaka. La création d'objets garnis de perles à Dumazulu (À GAUCHE) fait complètement partie de la culture zouloue.

Mit Holzkeulen, langen Stöcken und Schilden bewaffnet, stehen diese Zulu-krieger (GEGENÜBER) zum Kriegstanz bereit. Shakaland ist ein Museumsdorf bei Eshowe, wo die vielgestaltigen Bräuche und Rituale der Zulu seit Shakas Zeiten gepflegt werden. Perlenschmuck, der in Dumazulu ange-fertigt wird (OBEN), ist ein integraler Bestandteil der Zulukultur.

119

FIELDS OF GOLD

A colourful field of sunflowers (ABOVE) turns the drab Free State countryside into a blazing tapestry of yellow and gold. Contrasting with nature's grand display are the bright African murals painted on the walls of this house (OPPOSITE) at a Basotho cultural village.

BASOTHO MURALS

Cette éclatante multitude de tournesols (CI-CONTRE) égaye la monotonie du Free State avec sa tapisserie d'or et de jaune. Contrastant avec cette beauté de la nature, on découvre les motifs ethniques africains bariolés sur les murs de cette maison (CI-DESSUS) dans un village culturel basotho.

Ein fröhliches Sonnenblumenfeld (GEGENÜBER) verändert die eintönige Landschaft im Freistaat in ein leuchtendes Bild in Gelb und Gold. Die bunten afrikanischen Motive, die diese Hauswände in einem Museumsdorf der Basotho zieren (OBEN), ergänzen die großartige Naturschönheit.

BREWING TRADITIONAL BEER

Basotho women at the cultural village grind maize, brew beer and decorate their homesteads, as they have done for 400 years.

———————

Ces femmes en costume traditionnel basotho, moulent du maïs, brassent de la bière et décorent leurs demeures, suivant une tradition qui remonte à 400 ans.

———————

Basothofrauen in traditioneller Kleidung stampfen Mais, brauen Bier und verzieren ihre Heimstätte, ganz so, wie sie es seit 400 Jahren tun.

VILLAGE LIFE

GOLDEN GATE HIGHLANDS NATIONAL PARK

Eroded by wind and water, sandstone sentinels flank the grasslands of Golden Gate (ABOVE), a beautiful montane retreat (OPPOSITE).

Erodées par les éléments, ces sentinelles de grès bordent les prairies du Golden Gate (CI-DESSUS), un lieu de villégiature dans les montagnes (CI-CONTRE).

Von Wind und Wasser erodierte Sandsteinbastionen in den Grasflächen im Golden Gate (OBEN), einer herrlichen Berglandschaft (GEGENÜBER).

HORSE RIDING IN GOLDEN GATE

behtlehem

126

BETHLEHEM COUNTRYSIDE

Distant mountains form a brooding silhouette over country fields as storm clouds gather near Bethlehem (ABOVE) at the height of summer. To the south-west, like an oasis in the desert, the cool waters of Gariep Dam (OPPOSITE) offer tired travellers a scenic respite from the Free State's dusty plains.

GARIEP DAM

Les montagnes forment une silhouette menaçante à l'horizon, alors que des nuages orageux se rassemblent au-dessus des champs, près de Bethléem (CI-CONTRE). Dans le Sud-Ouest, les eaux fraîches du Gariep Dam (CI-DESSUS), comme une oasis dans le désert, présentent aux voyageurs fatigués un répit des plaines poussiéreuses du Free State.

In der Nähe von Bethlehem brüten die Berge im Hintergrund der Ländereien, über denen sich sommerliche Gewitterwolken bilden (GEGENÜBER). Im Südwesten nimmt sich der Gariep Stausee (OBEN) wie eine Oase aus und bietet dem müden Reisenden eine landschaftliche Erquickung inmitten den staubigen Ebenen im Freistaat.

TROUT FISHING

Revelling in the tranquillity of a day in the country, a trout fisherman finds solitude on the sylvan banks of a small dam (ABOVE), near Dullstroom. Wild cosmos blooms (OPPOSITE) turn the high Mpumalanga grasslands near Middelburg into a riot of colour.

COSMOS BLOOMS

Sur la rive boisée d'un petit lac près de Dullstroom (CI-CONTRE), un pêcheur de truite profite au mieux de la tranquillité d'une journée à la campagne. Ces cosmos sauvages (CI-DESSUS) transforment les plaines herbeuses du Mpumalanga près de Middelburg, en une tapisserie bariolée de couleurs.

Am malerischen Seeufer genießt ein Forellenangler die Geruhsamkeit der friedlichen Umgebung bei Dullstroom (GEGENÜBER). Wilde Kosmos (OBEN) verleihen der Grassteppe in Mpumalanga ein farbenfreudiges Aussehen.

NDEBELE CULTURAL VILLAGE

NDEBELE MURALS

Ndebele women wearing traditional neckrings and blankets (OPPOSITE). Bright colours are painstakingly applied to the walls of a house (ABOVE).

Femmes Ndebele portant les traditionnels anneaux et la couverture (CI-CONTRE). Les murs sont minutieusement peints de couleurs vives (CI-DESSUS).

Ndebele Frauen in ihren traditionellen Halsringen und Decken (GEGENÜBER). Die Hauswände werden mit viel Mühe mit bunten Farben verziert (OBEN).

ROBBER'S PASS

A nostalgic walk through the prospectors' village of Pilgrim's Rest in Mpumalanga (OPPOSITE) recalls the heady days of the gold-rush, when the highlands teemed with diggers and panners who risked their lives bearing the yellow metal back to the big cities along tortuous tracks like Robber's Pass – now a tarred road (ABOVE). Today Pilgrim's Rest is a national monument.

PILGRIM'S REST, NATIONAL MONUMENT

Une balade nostalgique dans le village de Pilgrim's Rest au Mpumalanga (CI-DESSUS) évoque l'époque grisante de la ruée vers l'or, quand les collines fourmillaient de prospecteurs qui risquaient leur vie en transportant l'or vers les grandes villes, empruntant des pistes tortueuses comme celle de Robber's Pass (CI-CONTRE), maintenant une route macadamisée. Pilgrim's Rest a été déclaré un monument national.

Ein nostalgischer Spaziergang durch das Goldgräberdorf Pilgrim's Rest in Mpumalanga (OBEN), das unter Denkmalschutz steht, erinnert an die Zeit des Goldrausches, als die Hochebenen von Schürfern und Bergleuten wimmelten, die ihr Leben aufs Spiel setzten, um das gelbe Metall in die großen Städte zu bringen und über mühsame Bergwege ziehen mußten, wie den Räuberpass, der jetzt eine Asphaltstraße ist (GEGENÜBER).

BERLIN FALLS

A cascade of white water plummets over a cliff into the bush-fringed dam at Berlin Falls near Graskop (ABOVE), while a helicopter hovers overhead. The scouring action over the centuries of the Motlatse and Sefogane rivers has created a moonscape of weird and wonderful forms in the rocks, which is known as Bourke's Luck Potholes (OPPOSITE).

BOURKE'S LUCK POTHOLES

Près de Graskop, une cascade d'eau bouillonnante dévale les Berlin Falls dans un étang bordé de broussailles (CI-CONTRE), alors qu'un hélicoptère fait du surplace au-dessus. Des siècles d'érosion constante par le cours de la Motlatse et de la Sefogane ont créé un paysage lunaire aux étranges formations rocheuses, appelé Bourke's Luck Potholes (CI-DESSUS).

Das schäumende Wasser stürzt über eine Felswand in den von Sträuchern umringten Stausee und bildet die Berlin-Fälle in der Nähe von Graskop (GEGENÜBER). Ein Hubschrauber kreist über dem Naturschauspiel. Über Jahrhunderte haben die Flüsse, Motlatse und Sefogane, durch Felsverspülungen eine schauerlich-schöne Mondlandschaft in den Felsenwänden geformt, die als Bourke's Luck Potholes bekannt ist (OBEN).

blyde river canyon

136

BLYDEPOORT DAM

THREE RONDAVELS

Like stately sentinels presiding over a priceless kingdom, the bush-fringed turrets of the Three Rondavels (LEFT) loom above the Blydepoort Dam and Blyde River Canyon (OPPOSITE), one of the scenic wonders of southern Africa.

Comme les gardiennes d'un trésor inestimable surgissant de la brousse qui les entoure, les tourelles des Three Rondavels surplombent le Blydepoort Dam (À GAUCHE) et le Blyde River Canyon (CI-CONTRE), un des grandioses panoramas d'Afrique australe.

Wie majestätische Wächter postieren sich die Felstürme der Drei Rondavels (Rundhütten) über dem Blydepoort Stausee (LINKS) und dem Blyde River Cañon (GEGENÜBER), der eines der beeindruckendsten Landschaftspanoramen im südlichen Afrika bietet.

137

BUFFELSHOEK PRIVATE NATURE RESERVE

The magic of the wild has been preserved in Bushveld sanctuaries such as Buffelshoek in the Sabi Sand Reserve (ABOVE), where elephants and a huge variety of other animals have right of way, and at Olifants River Rest Camp in the Kruger National Park (OPPOSITE), where the Sabi River makes its way through the bush towards the horizons of old Africa.

OLIFANTS RIVER REST CAMP

L'enchantement de la nature indomptée a été préservé dans les sanctuaires du Bushveld, comme à la Sabi Sand Reserve (CI-CONTRE), où les éléphants et une énorme variété d'autres animaux ont la priorité, et à l'Oliphants River Rest Camp dans le Kruger National Park (CI-DESSUS) où la Sabi se faufile entre les broussailles, vers l'horizon de l'Afrique éternelle.

Der Zauber der naturbelassenen Wildnis wird in Schutzgebieten in der Buschsavanne, wie Buffelshoek im Sabi Sand Wildpark (GEGENÜBER) erhalten, wo Elefanten und eine Vielzahl anderer Tiere sich ungehindert bewegen können, und auch im Olifants River Rastlager im Kruger Nationalpark (OBEN), wo der Sabi-Fluß sich durch die Landschaft schlängelt zu den fernen Horizonten des ursprünglichen Afrika.

LEOPARD, FEARSOME PREDATOR

The cryptic grace of a solitary killer is captured perfectly by this picture of a leopard resting in the fork of a tree (ABOVE). A male lion in the Kruger National Park (OPPOSITE) shows the battle scars and the bloodied jaws, teeth and mane that make it the most feared cat on earth. In spite of their ferocious appearance, lions rely on the females to do most of the hunting.

LION, KING OF THE BEASTS

L'expression énigmatique d'un tueur solitaire a été capturée à la perfection dans cette photo d'un léopard au repos dans un arbre (CI-CONTRE). Au Kruger PARK (CI-DESSUS), un lion couvert de cicatrices, avec la mâchoire, les dents et la crinière sanglantes, démontre qu'il est le félin le plus redouté sur terre. Malgré la férocité apparente des lions mâles, ce sont les femelles qui s'occupent le plus souvent de la chasse.

Die geheimnisvolle Anmut des einsamen Jägers ist in diesem Bild eines Leoparden, der in einer Baumgabel ruht, vollendet eingefangen (GEGENÜBER). Ein Löwe im Kruger Nationalpark (OBEN) zeigt die blutigen Lefzen und Zähne, die struppige Mähne und die Narben überstandener Kämpfe, die ihn zur meist gefürchteten Raubkatze der Erde machen. Dabei verläßt sich der Löwe beim Jagen überwiegend auf die Weibchen.

NIGHT DRIVE, KRUGER

As the russet colours of sunset descend on the Kruger National Park, a game warden heads into the bush with a cargo of game-watchers (ABOVE), eager to see the inhabitants of one of the world's most prolific animal sanctuaries. Statuesque among the trees of the Sabi Sand Reserve, a giraffe (OPPOSITE) suns itself in the golden rays of winter sun.

GIRAFFE, SABI SAND RESERVE

Sous le ciel rouge du crépuscule, un guide mène dans la brousse du Kruger National Park (CI-CONTRE) un groupe de touristes avides d'observer les résidents d'une des réserves d'animaux des plus abondantes du monde. Entre les arbres de la Sabi Sand Reserve, une girafe (CI-DESSUS) se réchauffe dans les rayons du soleil hivernal.

Im Schein der Abenddämmerung bricht ein Wildwart im Kruger National-park zur Pirschfahrt auf mit seiner Gruppe von Wildbeobachtern (GEGENÜBER), die erpicht darauf sind, den Bewohnern eines Wildschutz-gebiets zu begegnen, das für seinen Reichtum an Tierleben weltbekannt ist. Die grazil aufragende Gestalt einer Giraffe zwischen den Bäumen im Sabi Sands Wildpark (OBEN), die sich in der Wintersonne wärmt.

KRUGER WATERHOLE

Cape buffalo cool off at a waterhole (ABOVE) in the Kruger National Park, home to nearly 22,000 of these magnificent horned mammals. The Kruger is Africa's oldest and one of the world's greatest game reserves, renowned for the beauty of its rustic bush camps, abundant game and ancient ruins, such as the Thulamela Ruins (OPPOSITE), which date back to the 12th century.

THULAMELA RUINS, KRUGER

Un troupeau de buffles se rafraîchit à un point d'eau (CI-CONTRE) dans le Kruger National Park. Celui-ci contient près de 22,000 de ces splendides mammifères. Le Kruger est la plus ancienne réserve d'animaux en Afrique, et une des plus remarquables du monde. Il est réputé non seulement pour sa faune abondante, mais aussi pour ses ruines anciennes, comme les Thumela Ruins (CI-DESSUS), qui remontent au 12ième siècle.

Afrikanische Büffel verschaffen sich Kühlung in einem Wasserloch im Kruger Nationalpark (GEGENÜBER), wo nahezu 22,000 dieser imposant gehörnten Säugetiere beheimatet sind. Der Kruger Nationalpark ist das älteste Wildschutzgebiet in Afrika und dazu eines der größten der Welt. Der Wildpark ist berühmt für schöne Rastlager, die große Anzahl an Wild und auch für alte Ruinen, wie die Thulamela Ruinen (OBEN).

THOHOYANDOU TEA PLANTATION

BAOBABS, MUSSINA NATURE RESERVE

The gentle lines of a tea plantation near Thohoyandou (OPPOSITE) contrasts with these contorted baobab trees (ABOVE).

Les contours apaisants d'une plantation de thé près de Thohoyandou (CI-CONTRE), contrastent avec les lignes tourmentées de ces baobabs (CI-DESSUS).

Die sanften Hänge einer Teeplantage bei Thohoyandou (GEGENÜBER) bilden einen starken Kontrast zu diesen verschlungenen Affenbrotbäumen (OBEN).

NIGHT LIGHTS, MELVILLE

The bright lights of Melville (ABOVE) invite revellers to relax into the early hours, while lights of a different kind illuminate downtown Johannesburg (OPPOSITE).

Les lumières de Melville invitent les couche-tard jusqu'aux petites heures (CI-DESSUS). Une lumière d'une autre qualité baigne Johannesburg (CI-CONTRE).

Hell erleuchtete Fassaden in Mellville locken Nachtschwärmer (OBEN), während in der Innenstadt von Johannesburg (GEGENÜBER) andere Lichter blinken.

SUNSET OVER HILLBROW

NELSON MANDELA BRIDGE

The Nelson Mandela Bridge (ABOVE) gives access to a rejuvenated city centre. Melrose Arch (OPPOSITE) where the trendy set meet.

Le Nelson Mandela Bridge (CI-DESSUS) voie d'accès au centre ville rénové. Melrose Arch (CI-CONTRE) un rendez-vous à la mode.

Die Nelson-Mandela-Brücke (OBEN) führt in das neu gestaltete Stadtzentrum. Melrose Arch (GEGENÜBER), wo sich die Schickeria trifft.

MELROSE ARCH

152

A passerby seems oblivious to the gaudy mural advertising a local brew (RIGHT). With ingenuity, colour and the help of a makeshift drummer, a busker sings for his supper at the craft market outside MuseumAfrica (OPPOSITE).

NEWTOWN MURAL

PAVEMENT MINSTREL

Un passant blasé, ignore la publicité tape-à-l'œil pour une bière locale (CI-CONTRE). Avec un peu d'ingéniosité, de la couleur et un batteur improvisé, un musicien ambulant fait son numéro à un marché artisanal près du Museum Africa (À GAUCHE).

153

Ein vorübergehender Passant scheint die grelle Wandbemalung, Werbung für ein einheimisches Bier, gar nicht wahrzunehmen (GEGENÜBER). Mit Einfallsreichtum, etwas Farbe und der Hilfe eines Behelfstrommlers, hofft dieser Straßensänger auf dem Markt vor dem Museum Africa etwas Geld zu verdienen (LINKS).

KIM SACKS ART GALLERY

Arts, curios and crafts from all over Africa are showcased at the Kim Sacks
Art Gallery in Parkwood (ABOVE). A glittering array of copper pots, pans and
other fascinating trinkets from various parts of Asia pack the tables of this
vendor (OPPOSITE) at the Oriental Plaza.

ORIENTAL PLAZA

Oeuvres d'art, souvenirs et objets artisanaux originaires de l'Afrique entière sont exposés chez Kim Sacks Art Gallery à Parkwood (CI-CONTRE). Une gamme scintillante de pots de cuivre, poêles et autres bibelots intrigants venant d'Asie, remplit cet étalage à l'Oriental Plaza (CI-DESSUS).

Kunstgegenstände, Andenken und Kunstgewerbliches aus ganz Afrika werden in der Kim Sacks Kunstgalerie in Parkwood ausgestellt (GEGENÜBER). Blitzende Kupfergefässe und andere faszinierende Gegenstände aus verschiedenen asiatischen Ländern drängen sich auf den Tischen dieses Händlers (OBEN) auf dem orientalischen Markt.

SANDTON SQUARE

The upmarket shops, restaurants, cinema complexes and elegant malls of Sandton Square (LEFT) contrast with the informality of outdoor African craft stalls at Sandton's Village Walk Shopping Centre (OPPOSITE).

Les magasins haut-de-gamme, restaurants, complexes multisalles et les élégants centres commerciaux de Sandton Square (À GAUCHE) contrastent fortement avec l'atmosphère décontractée de ce marché en plein air d'artisanat africain, au Village Walk Shopping Centre de Sandton (CI-CONTRE).

Die vornehmen Geschäfte, Restaurants und Kinos und die eleganten Passagen im Sandton Square (LINKS) bilden einen Gegensatz zu den einfachen Ständen mit afrikanischen Handarbeiten, die im Village Walk Einkaufszentrum in Sandton angeboten werden (GEGENÜBER).

VILLAGE WALK SHOPPING CENTRE

APARTHEID MUSEUM

GOLD REEF CITY

The Apartheid Museum (OPPOSITE), a reminder of our nation's past. Gold Reef City (ABOVE) recalls the Witwatersrand gold rush era.

L'Apartheid Museum (CI-CONTRE) un rappel du passé de notre pays. Gold Reef City (CI-DESSUS) évoque l'ère de la ruée vers l'or.

Das Apartheid Museum (GEGENÜBER) erinnert an die Vergangenheit der Nation und Gold Reef City (OBEN) an die Goldrauschära.

MANDELA HOUSE MUSEUM, SOWETO

Poignant memorabilia (ABOVE) recall the life and times of Nelson Mandela at the tiny Orlando West home he shared with his former wife, Winnie, before his arrest on treason charges. The house has been converted into a museum and, together with Wandie's Place (OPPOSITE), is a major tourist attraction for first-time visitors to Soweto.

WANDIE'S PLACE, SOWETO

La vie et l'époque de Nelson Mandela sont évoqués par ces souvenirs poignants à la petite maison d'Orlando West, qu'il habitait avec sa première épouse Winnie, avant son arrestation pour trahison (CI-CONTRE). La maison a été transformée en musée, et, avec Wandie's Place (CI-DESSUS), est une importante attraction touristique de Soweto.

Ergreifende Erinnerungsstücke (GEGENÜBER) rufen den Lebensabschnitt von Nelson Mandela ins Gedächtnis, als er mit seiner ehemaligen Frau, Winnie, in dem kleine Haus in Orlando West lebte, ehe er wegen Hochverrat inhaftiert wurde. Das Haus ist jetzt ein Museum und bedeutet – ebenso wie Wandie's Place (OBEN) – eine wichtige Touristenattraktion für Besucher, die zum ersten Mal nach Soweto kommen.

SOWETO STREET MARKET

Informal stalls have mushroomed on the streets of Soweto (ABOVE), where you can haggle with traders for just about anything, from a chocolate bar to a Persian carpet or a range of African crafts. Every day this trader at the Baragwanath Taxi Rank (OPPOSITE) unloads his sacks of medicinal herbs and bulbs, and sells them without the luxury of a stall or props.

BARAGWANATH TAXI RANK HAWKER

Les échoppes prolifèrent à Soweto (CI-CONTRE), où il est possible de marchander avec les propriétaires pour tout ce qui est à l'étalage, d'un chocolat à un tapis persan en passant par des objets d'artisanat. Se passant du luxe d'un stand ou autres accessoires, ce marchand vend ses herbes médicinales à la station de taxi de Baragwanath (CI-DESSUS).

Straßenstände sind in Soweto wie Pilze aus der Erde geschossen (GEGENÜBER). Man feilscht mit den Händlern um alles Erdenkliche, von einer Tafel Schokolade bis zu einem Perserteppich oder afrikanischen Handarbeiten. Tagtäglich lädt dieser Händler am Taxenstand des Baragwanath Krankenhauses seine Säcke mit Heilkräutern und – knollen ab und verkauft sie ohne jeden Stand oder Stellagen (OBEN).

ARDENT FOOTBALL SUPPORTER

FNB STADIUM, SOWETO

Soccer mania rules every weekend in Soweto, when enthusiastic fans (OPPOSITE) flock to the FNB Stadium (ABOVE).

La folie du football règne à Soweto au week-end, quand les supporters (CI-CONTRE) envahissent le FNB Stadium (CI-DESSUS).

Jedes Wochenende grassiert Fußballfieber in Soweto, wenn begeisterte Fans (GEGENÜBER) das FNB Stadium füllen (OBEN).

pretoria

166

UNION BUILDINGS

DELVILLE WOOD MEMORIAL

Floodlights accentuate the palatial grandeur of Herbert Baker's Union Buildings in Pretoria (OPPOSITE). Within the grounds the Delville Wood Memorial (LEFT) honours South African troops who died during the two world wars.

L'harmonie de l'Union Building à Pretoria, œuvre de Herbert Baker, est mise en valeur par les illuminations (CI-CONTRE). Tout proche, le Delville Wood Memorial (À GAUCHE) rend hommage aux troupes sud africaines qui périrent durant les deux Guerres mondiales.

Scheinwerfer unterstreichen die palastartige Erhabenheit der Unionsgebäude in Pretoria, die von dem Architekten, Herbert Baker, stammen (GEGENÜBER). In den Anlagen steht auch das Denkmal von Delville Wood (LINKS), das der gefallenen südafrikanischen Truppen im Ersten Weltkrieg gedenkt.

167

JACARANDA EXTRAVAGANZA

Every October the blooms of 70,000 jacaranda trees (LEFT) cloak the city of Pretoria in a brilliant carpet of mauve. Another of Pretoria's attractions is Melrose House (OPPOSITE), one of South Africa's finest showcases of Victoriana, in which the Vereeniging Treaty was signed in 1902.

Chaque année au mois d'octobre, les fleurs de 70,000 jacarandas (À GAUCHE) recouvrent la cité de Pretoria d'un tapis au mauve éclatant. Une autre attraction de la ville est Melrose Court (CI-CONTRE), un des plus remarquables exemples de style victorien en Afrique du Sud, où, en 1902, fut signé le traité de Vereeniging.

Alljährlich blühen im Oktober 70,000 Jakarandabäume (LINKS) in Pretoria und hüllen die Stadt in einen lila Blüten-mantel. Eine weitere Attraktion von Pretoria ist Melrose-Haus (GEGENÜBER), eines der schönsten, viktorianischen Häuser in Südafrika, wo 1902 das Friedensabkommen von Vereeniging unterzeichnet wurde.

MELROSE HOUSE

NYAMA CHOMA, LESEDI

Dancers at Lesedi Cultural Village (ABOVE) in the Magaliesberg welcome visitors before they feast at the Nyama Choma restaurant, while a Zulu musician (OPPOSITE) performs in traditional attire. The village is inhabited by four different ethnic groups: Xhosa, Pedi, Zulu and Basotho people.

LESEDI MUSICIAN

Des danseurs au Lesedi Cultural Village dans le Magaliesberg (CI-CONTRE), accueillent les visiteurs avant qu'ils ne se régalent au restaurant Nyama Choma. Un musicien Zoulou en costume traditionnel (À DROITE). Le village est habité par quatre groupes ethniques: Xhosa, Pedi, Zoulou et Basotho.

Diese Tänzer im Lesedi Museumsdorf in den Magaliesbergen (GEGENÜBER) begrüßen die Besucher, ehe sie dann im Nyoma Choma Restaurant speisen. Ein Zulu Musikant (RECHTS) in traditioneller Tracht. Das Museumsdorf beherbergt vier verschiedene Volksgruppen: Xhosa, Pedi, Zulu und Basotho.

171

HARTBEESPOORT DAM

BALLOONING, MAGALIESBERG

Sunset suffuses the shoreline of Hartbeespoort Dam with a palette of crimson hues (OPPOSITE). Gaily coloured hot-air balloons (LEFT) ascend into the crisp Highveld air of the Magaliesberg near Pretoria.

Le soleil couchant teint la rive de Hartbeespoort Dam dans une gamme de tons pourpres (CI-CONTRE). Au Magaliesberg, près de Pretoria, des montgolfières aux couleurs vives (À GAUCHE), montent dans l'air piquant du Highveld.

Der Sonnenuntergang taucht die Ufer des Hartbeespoort Stausees in eine Palette rötlicher Farbschattierungen (GEGENÜBER). Bunte Heißluftballons (LINKS) steigen in die kühle Luft der Hochebene bei den Magaliesbergen in der Nähe von Pretoria empor.

173

PALACE OF THE LOST CITY

Ornate domes and boulevards surrounded by water beckon visitors to enter the 'legendary' Palace of the Lost City (ABOVE), one of the most spectacular entertainment centres and hotels in Africa, situated in the folds of the Magaliesberg north of Rustenburg. One of the premier attractions of the Palace is its idyllic man-made beach (OPPOSITE).

WAVE POOL, LOST CITY

Les dômes richement ornés du légendaire 'Palace of the Lost City' situé dans les replis du Magaliesberg au nord de Rustenburg (CI-CONTRE), attirent les visiteurs dans un des parcs de loisirs des plus spectaculaires en Afrique. Une des plus grosses attractions du parc est l'idyllique plage artificielle (CI-DESSUS).

Prunkvolle Kuppeln und einladende Boulevards am Wasser empfangen den Besucher des 'legendären' Palace of the Lost City (GEGENÜBER), eines der anspruchsvollsten Kasino-, Unterhaltungs- und Hotelkomplexe in ganz Afrika, das in den Magaliesbergen, nördlich von Rustenburg, liegt. Zu den Hauptattraktionen dieser Anlagen zahlt der idyllische, künstlich angelegte Strand (OBEN).

176

ELEPHANT, PILANESBERG NATIONAL PARK

The Pilanesberg National Park, a two-hour drive north of Johannesburg, is home to over 8,000 animals including the Big Five.

Le Pilanesberg National Park, à deux heures de Johannesburg, est l'habitat de plus de 8,000 animaux, y compris les grands fauves.

Der Pilanesberg Nationalpark, nur zwei Autostunden von Johannesburg entfernt, beheimatet mehr als 8,000 Tiere, einschließlich der 'Großen Fünf'.